ZOROASTRIANISM

Zoroastrianism
A Beleaguered Faith

Cyrus R Pangborn

ADVENT BOOKS New York

© Cyrus R. Pangborn, 1983

ISBN 0-89891-006-4

Library of Congress Catalog Card # ᐟ   82-074483

This First Edition is published in the United States of America
by special arrangement with
Vikas Publishing House Pvt Ltd, New Delhi, India.

Printed in India

To My Family
for whom, as for me, a sojourn in India
was an experience in learning that despite
the poignant fragility of life, one can
again and again be surprised by joy.

Contents

Foreword

"Of all the great religions of the world Zoroastrianism was the least well served." (Zaehner) The dictum is apt if it is understood as meaning simply that its leaders, after Zoroaster, lacked the stature and the vision to foster creative evolution for the religion in good times with the same earnestness demonstrated in averting its extinction in times of crisis.

The dictum can also by extension refer to neglect of Zoroastrianism by chroniclers of the world's religions. Of the many textbooks written for those engaged in historical or comparative religious study, only a few include accounts of Zoroastrianism; and even their treatments in most instances are so condensed as to be of little value. At best they serve merely to arouse a curiosity which they then fail to satisfy. (I am not, of course, referring here to specialized scholarly works of history, biography, anthropology, and philology. There have been many of these but they are not the treatments that make general knowledge accessible to collegians or other literate and inquiring readers.)

The initial motive I had for engaging in the task of writing the account which follows was to remedy this deficiency. The historians may argue that Zoroastrians are so few in number that their religion deserves only slight attention, but the inherent worth of many a tenet of Zoroastrianism, the intriguing uniqueness of certain of its beliefs and practices, and the very fact that it *has* survived justify a chronicle of greater length and depth than cursory summation provides—a work that can be listed on a course syllabus for collateral reading or read independently by anyone interested in Iranian and Indian cultural history.

Once launched, the project acquired added impetus from discovering that Zoroastrians themselves were as eager to read a disinterested account as I was to write it. They are the many to whom I owe gratitude for encouragement and information. Among them are a smaller but still generous number of scholars, priests, institutional administrators, and well-informed lay people whose knowledge and experience make them expert informants. Representing communities in India, Iran, England, Canada, and the USA, every

one of them deserves mention. Discretion, however, requires that
the list be limited to principal advisers. For the careful reading each
gave to all or part of the manuscript, and for the corrections and
revisions recommended, I am especially grateful to Dastur
Kaikhusroo M. JamaspAsa, Joint Honorary Secretary of the K.R.
Cama Oriental Institute, Bombay; Ervad Maneck F. Kanga, former-
ly Professor of Avestan Language and Literature, the Universities of
Poona and Bombay; Dastur Dr. Firoze M. Kotwal, H.B. Wadia
Atash Behram (Fire-Temple), Bombay; and Jehangir R. Patel,
Editor of *Parsiana*, Bombay. Others to whom I am indebted for
indispensable advice on treating several issues, technical as well as
practical, are Dr. Hanns-Peter Schmidt, Professor of Near Eastern
Languages, University of California (Los Angeles), and H. E.
Eduljee, Joint Honorary Secretary of the K.R. Cama Oriental Insti-
tute, Bombay. Such faults as remain despite their endeavors are
those for which I alone remain responsible.

As for the hope that has sustained my own endeavors, it is that
the religion of Zoroaster may be rescued from benign neglect and
find acceptance as one deservedly included among the living religions of the world.

New Brunswick, New Jersey   CYRUS R. PANGBORN

Explanations

Terms

A work such as this requires using many names of terms foreign to the readers of English for whom it is intended. Most of such terms appear in a variety of forms in written sources as a consequence of the evolution of languages themselves and of alterations that are made when they are grafted on to another language altogether. That is to say, terms rooted in languages originating and developing in Iran have not only been subject, there, to change, but have also been adopted or adapted by latter-day Zoroastrians, the great majority of whom communicate in Gujarati and/or English. The questions of how to treat this variety and of whether to involve the press in using diacritical marks of certain letters different in form from their nearest equivalents in the English alphabet have been resolved in favor of the general reader by deciding which form of any given term seems to be most frequently used and therefore most familiar to contemporary Zoroastrians. If the protests of purists require response, it is that the work is not an exercise in philology; it is a story.

Abbreviations

JOURNALS

BSOAS *Bulletin of the School of Oriental and African Studies*
JAAR *Journal of the American Academy of Religion*
JCOI *Journal of the K.R. Cama Oriental Institute*

BOOKS

Dawn and Twilight *The Dawn and Twilight of Zoroastrianism,* R.C. Zaehner

Hand-Book *A Hand-Book of Information on Zoroastrianism,* Khurshed S. Dabu

History I *The History of Zoroastrianism*, Vol. I, Mary Boyce

"*A Last Stronghold*"	"A Last Stronghold of Traditional Zoroastrianism," Mary Boyce
History	*History of Zoroastrianism*, Maneckji N. Dhalla
HR II	*Historia Religionum*, Vol. II, *Religions of the Present*
RCCP	*The Religious Ceremonies and Customs of the Parsees*, Jivanji Jamshedji Modi

Who the Zoroastrians Are

Zoroastrianism is today a worldwide phenomenon, for there is scarcely a continent where Zoroastrians cannot be found confessing their fidelity to Zoroaster, the prophet of ancient Iran. Such universality for the religion is not, however, widely recognized. Students of ancient history identify the religion in their minds mainly with Iranians of pre-Muslim times. Indologists tend to think that the Parsis of India are the only surviving Zoroastrians of the Common Era. The effect in the first instance is to invite the inference that there are no contemporary Iranian Zoroastrians, and in the second, to suggest that twentieth century Zoroastrians and Parsis are one and the same.

Of the two notions, the second borrows at least some plausibility from the fact that the Parsis of India do indeed represent well over half of all living Zoroastrians and are congregated in a few sizable and therefore easily visible communities of India. Their cohesion has aided them in the nurture of a sense of their common identity and the maintenance of uniform practices. It is tempting to think, therefore, that Parsi Zoroastrianism is normative Zoroastrianism and that it does not really matter very much if no distinction is made between the Parsi majority and the minority that is other than Parsi.

All this makes it important to set things straight at the outset by saying who the Zoroastrians are and where to find them. Once identified, their character—as revealed by the history and substance of the religion they profess—will be the easier to discern.[1]

---

[1] Several standard works sketch all or selected periods of the Zoroastrians' history, but always with regret expressed that surmise must do service for many a fact. See—for much of what can be known or believed—Maneckji Nusservanji Dhalla, *History of Zoroastrianism* (New York: Oxford University Press, 1938); A.V.W. Jackson, *Zoroaster, The Prophet of Ancient Iran* (New York:

The earliest Zoroastrians were simply Indo-Iranians who embraced the ideas of Zarathustra (Greek: Zoroaster). The traditional Indo-Iranian religion was polytheistic. Zoroaster sought its revision and reform, claiming that there is one supreme deity, Ahura Mazda, whose nature and will required changes in men's thought, worship, and mode of life. Once launched, the reformation made its way slowly across Iran to become eventually, as the good Mazdayasnian religion, the official creed of the late Achaemenid kings.

The Greek and Parthian eras, spanning the years from 330 B.C. to 250 B.C. and 250 B.C. to A.D. 226, were, respectively, destructive and half-heartedly supportive of Mazdayasnian religion, but recovery was sponsored by the Sasanids who, like the Achaemenids, hailed from the province of Pars (Fars: Persia). Unfortunately, this would not mark the end of troubles. The successful Muslim conquest in the seventh century was not immediately disastrous for the followers of Zoroaster, but for the last thousand of the next 1200 years their status was to be that of second-class subject, sometimes tolerated, often persecuted, and almost always harassed by Muslims seeking their conversion. A few thousands survived by congregating in remote areas where weather was harsh and life precarious. But the strategy more conducive to survival was emigration. The thousands who found refuge in Gujarat and prospered, and then in growing numbers gravitated to Bombay where they found favor with the English administration, were called Parsis—after the province which had already provided an alternate name for Iran itself.[2] It is their descendants who today constitute the great majority of the Zoroastrian fold, and who mainly during the twentieth century have established self-conscious communities not only in many another

Columbia University Press, 1898); R.C. Zaehner, *The Dawn and Twilight of Zoroastrianism* (New York: G.P. Putnam's Sons, 1961); I.J.S. Taraporewala, *The Religion of Zarathushtra* (Bombay: B.I. Taraporewala, 1965); Dosabhai Framji Karaka, *History of the Parsis*, Vol. I (London: Macmillan and Co., 1884).

[2]Wm. Theodore de Bary, et al. (compilers), *Sources of Tradition* (New York: Columbia University Press, 1958), Vol. LVI of *Records of Civilization, Sources and Studies,* ed. Jacques Barzun. The Parsis are described as the Indian community "most willing to do business . . . with the Europeans" since "they were bound neither by caste rules nor by prejudice against taking interest on loans . . ." and so could engage in the trade that enabled them to become "the most Westernized and the wealthiest single community in India." p. 664.

Indian city but elsewhere in Asia, in Africa, and in virtually every country of the English-speaking world.

The Indian Parsis' majority status among Zoroastrians, however, does not mean that their understanding and practice of the religion need be regarded as forever normative. For reasons to be identified later, the Parsis came to regard some of their religious traditions and religio-social customs as sacrosanct. This made it difficult for them to engage in the kind of conscious reconstruction that effectively combines the value of both continuity and adaptability.

Such traditionalism, by preserving much of the original pastoral character of the religion for a people now largely urban, has finally occasioned some erosion of zeal for religious practice. The Parsis' socio-economic status has also deteriorated over the past fifty years.[3] Worse, as a reason for anxiety, is the fact that in recent times there has been a loss in absolute numbers of Parsis of 10% per decade.[4]

Meanwhile, the Zoroastrians of Iran and the West have prospered. One might even say that those of Iran have been experiencing a renaissance. Encouraged by such factors as the guarantee of religious freedom, a modest increase in number of immigrant Parsis, and a willingness to accept converts, their numbers have increased by approximately 40% in little more than a decade.[5] During the same period, Zoroastrians in the West have increased in number from about 2,500 to perhaps as many as 5,000 or 6,000. The increment consists mainly of immigrant Parsis from India, but in their new Western settings the awareness of this chiefly-ethnic factor in identity is fading. Similarly, the authority of custom is waning in the face of an evident revival of concern to know "what Zoroaster really taught." It is really not numbers, therefore, but the

[3]See Sapur Faredun Desai, *A Community at the Cross-Road* (Bombay: New Book Co., Ltd., 1948), pp. 14-15, or P.A. Wadia, with the collaboration of Sheroo Mehta, Nergesh Sidhwa, Roshen Shroff, and Keki Randeria, *Parsis Ere the Shadows Thicken* (Bombay: P.A. Wadia, 1949), p. 4.

[4]For the decade of 1951-1961, census reports indicated a decline of the Parsi population in India from about 111,000 to 100,687. See Ervad Jal Rustamji Vimadalal, *What a Parsee Should Know* (Bombay: Mr. Justice Vimadalal, 1967), p. 17. By 1971, another decade later, the number had been reduced to 91,266, according to the Journal *Parsiana*, July 1972, p. 5.

[5]Iranian Zoroastrians numbered 21,000, according to the Census of 1966. The number estimated after the 1976 Census, on the basis of a preliminary tally, was 30,000. *Iran Almanac and Book of Facts, 1977,* 16th Edition (Tehran: The Echo of Iran Publisher, 1977).

adaptability and spirit of the communities outside of India that could qualify them for the role of saving the religion from extinction, or even for renewing and revivifying it as a living faith.

Every culture has its times of transition between ages, when one is dying and another is not yet born. Zoroastrians have known several such times "between the ages" when the exigencies of conquest and social unrest or turmoil have made existence precarious and survival dubious. Obviously, it is because they have survived these that we can speak of who they *are* rather than of who they *were*. What has been said so far, however, is, as it were, only a silhouette. To a description of the more discriminate features of this finally worldwide yet still beleaguered religious community, we must now turn.

CHAPTER 1

A Brief Chronicle of Zoroastrianism

Iran before Zoroaster

The pre-history of the Zoroastrians, as of all peoples, is obscure. We can know only those fragments of fact—or of legend pointing uncertainly back to facts—that memories succeeded in retaining until they could be preserved in writing. Obscurity, however, may derive not only from a dearth of facts, but from the variant versions of the few facts there are. Memory in a culture depending upon oral transmission can be honed to a fine point of accuracy, but it can also be immensely imaginative. Consequently, when attempting the reconstruction of the pre-history of a people, we find our resources are a confusing mixture of fact, legend, and myth.

The task of separating reasonably trustworthy Zoroastrian traditions from fanciful lore has been pursued now with increasing vigor over the last 200 years. Philologists, archaeologists, anthropologists, and historians have been the principal specialists, and it is the account as they have constructed it, with a large measure of agreement among themselves as to its plausibility, that is our present concern. The lore need not be left out, but the temptation to enter into debate about it with the credulous must be left to chroniclers whose interests permit it.

The Zoroastrians' ancestors, according to our sources, were migratory Indo-European tribes from the central Eurasian plain. Otherwise known as Aryas (Aryans), they were destined to provide the dominant genes and languages of the Greeks, Romans, Celts, Germans, and Slavs in Europe and of the Iranians and Indians in Asia.

In all probability, the Indo-Iranians were one of serveral multi-tribal groups composing the total Indo-European family. They and those of another group went two different if not entirely separate ways, some entering and giving their name to the area of Iran, while

the others (whom we know as the Indo-Aryans) invaded the sub-
continent, India.[1]

Further internal distinctions emerged as migration gave way to
more permanent settlements by regions and as each community
organized its life and culture according to its own experience.
Among the many such communities in Iran, we have heard most
perhaps about the Medes and the Persians, followed by the
Parthians, Bactrians, and Chorasmians. No one can be certain of
the time span required for this whole massive phenomenon of
migration, settlement, and acquisition of separate identities to run
its course, but its beginning may be placed near the end of the third
millennium.[2] Iran and India began to feel its impact by the middle
of the second millennium, which means that their pre-historical
and transitional period lasted roughly another thousand years.
The end of the era came with Cyrus the Great's "creation" of
Persia in the 6th century, for what he did was usher that part of
the world (east of the older Assyrian, Babylonian, Egyptian, and
Greek civilizations) into a new and historical age.[3]

[1]The evidence for the theory of a common origin comes from language and
religion. The large number of slightly different but often identical names for
both early Iranian and India's Vedic gods clearly indicates earlier association
of the two peoples within a single larger language group. The deities' characters were apt likewise to be similarly conceived, and there were features of ritual practices that we know were the same—or very nearly so—in both traditions.

[2]See A. T. Olmstead, *History of the Persian Empire* (Chicago: The University
of Chicago Press, 1948), pp. 10-11.

[3]*Ibid.* Olmstead notes the discovery of elementary writing by pictographs in
the area of the Iranian plateau before the arrival of the Indo-Iranians (p. 16)
and the use of cuneiform for writing Persian by the end of the 7th century B.C.
(p. 34). But until there is excavation of sites connected with the Median effort
of the 7th century to develop the first empire in that area (p. 33), we have no
evidence that writing was in regular use there—such as for royal recording—
until the time of Cyrus the Great. (Cyrus first came to notice in 599 B.C. as a
vassal in Persia for the Medes, then to prominence when he rebelled against
his overlords and founded the Persian Empire in 550. Twenty years before his
death in 530 B.C., his conquests had enabled him to put together "the greatest
empire yet known to history" (p. 59). Even then, Persian seems to have been
used only for royal inscriptions, and the bulk of our information for most of
the Achaemenid period is derived from tables showing the liberal use made of
the languages of subject peoples—Elamite, Akkadian, and Aramaic (p. 68).
There are, of course, the accounts written by visiting Greek historians such as
Herodotus and Strabo. But what they wrote about earlier times was what their

The Prophet

Zoroaster, the prophet by whose name the religion of Iran came principally to be known, is thought to have lived most of his adult life before "the new age." Lacking precise biographical data, we must rely upon what he himself recounted of his experiences in his hymns, the *Gathas*, and upon the ability of his immediate followers to memorize and recall them. References to places and persons seemed to early Western scholars to point to his having been born in western Iran "somewhere in Azarbaijan," but this is now disputed by authorities who think the land of his birth and youth was much to the east, and probably north of present-day Iran.[4] The ancestral name was Spitama; that is made certain by the Gathas, as are also the names of his father, Pourushaspa, and his mother, Dughdhova.

Dates for his birth and mission must be estimated by inference. Zoroaster cited Vishtaspa as his royal patron and first prestigious convert. The Zoroastrian tradition, as found in written works of the 9th century A.D., is that the Mazdayasnian religion[5] made its appearance 258 years before Alexander's conquest of 330 B.C. This reconstruction is too artificially contrived to be plausible, and scholars with greater appreciation of the time required for changes

---

informants knew of their accumulated oral tradition. We also have large portions of the *Avesta*, the Zoroastrian Scriptures, as a source, but even if the *Avesta* was in writing during Achaemenid times, there are no surviving copies dating from that period. Moreover, there is a certain amount of risk involved in trusting what it says about the pre-Achaemenid period, since one apparent purpose in composing it was to show that contemporary Zoroastrianism derived its authority from faithfully preserving older traditions. History *can* be re-written, when this interest is involved, to make the past agree with present realities. I do not quite fully share, therefore, Olmstead's confidence that as regards the relevant portions of the *Avesta*, "it still retains the essential features of this prehistoric culture" (p. 16).

[4]See A. V. Williams Jackson, *Zoroaster, The Prophet of Ancient Iran* (New York: Columbia University Press, 1898) p. 205. Jackson's inquiry was so exhaustive of sources and traditions that for a long time there was a general inclination to accept his view of where Zoroaster was born and of where he later went in search of followers. For a contemporary view now more widely accepted, see Mary Boyce, *The History of Zoroastrianism*, Vol. I (Leiden: E. J. Brill, 1975), p. 190 (cited hereafter as *History I*).

[5]The name, Mazdayasnian, for the religion of the worshippers of Mazda, became the common one for designating Zoroastrianism during Achaemenid times.

to occur in the languages and customs of traditionalist societies—
and with enough restraint to be satisfied with approximations—are
suggesting that Zoroaster may have been born in the mid-2nd
millennium B.C. at the earliest or near the beginning of the 1st
millennium at latest.[6]

It is with rather more certainty that we can describe Zoroaster's
early career as following a pattern common among religious innova-
tors. There was first the period of agonizing reflection. But when
new insights, experienced as divine revelation, resolved his doubts
and questions and inspired him to preach, he found himself a
prophet without honor in his own homeland. So began a frustrating
itinerant search for converts that bore no fruit (except for one
cousin who believed) until, having reached the Bactrian area of
Chorasmia in his wanderings and endured the persecution meted
out to him there by native priests and nobility, he finally won
acceptance from the reigning prince, Vishtaspa.

Success was his at last. The royal family and the court followed

[6]See, again, Boyce (*ibid.*), who is much respected by the Zoroastrians' own
scholars. Numerous Parsi writers, however, more renowned for their piety
and sincerity than for scholarship, have a penchant for evading the historical
problems and accepting as literal the mythical components of their tradition.
The Persians, in speculating about creation and their own pre-history, developed the idea of a creation that first brought the divine realm into being, then
the earthly realm, the latter patterned after the divine one. The whole process,
including the time it would take for history to run its course, was thought to
require 12,000 years, divided into four epochs of 3,000 years each. According to
this scheme, *fravashis*, the prototypal souls of men, were created to dwell in the
divine realm, to await there the eventual creation of their counterparts, the
souls of earthly men. Jackson concludes that the several Greek writers who
visited Persia in Achaemenid times and then chronicled Zoroaster's birth as
having occurred 6,000 years before the 5th century B.C. were confusing his
human birth with the creation of his fravashi two epochs earlier. (*Op. cit.*,
p. 152.) We now know, from comparative studies, that the appeal of early
dating for religious origins is well nigh universal. The closer the rise of traditions that men prize to the time of the world's creation, the purer and less
compromised by later corruptions they must be! Besides, the older the traditions are, the more they have surely demonstrated their truth—the power
sustaining their life and longevity! A work compiled by Naval Kavasjee D.
Naigamwalla, *Zarathushtra's Glorious Faith* (Poona, 1967), and consisting
mainly of passages quoted from works by other pious Parsis, unwittingly
illustrates precisely these motifs. It is a stunning example of authors having
reinforced one another by exchange of quotations and of mistaking repetition
of claims for competence in scholarship.

the prince, and with such patronage, Zoroaster had the encouragement he needed for further propagation of his reform. There were still holy wars to be fought against invading Turanians from the north, but by the time of Zoroaster's death (as a martyr during one such war, according to tradition), his reforming faith was spreading and on its way to becoming the national religion of Iran. Since details will come later, the only statement about the faith needful here is that it was a qualified monotheism critical of an old Aryan polytheism, a cultic reform that had no use for magic or respect for demonic forces, a religious ethic mandating perfectionist ideals of personal honesty and integrity, and a social ethic prudentially commending stewardship as the proper ideal for the more settled pastoral society before which the older and cruder tribal nomadism was only grudgingly giving way.

Rising and Falling Tides of Fortune

With the death of Zoroaster, the religion was never again to have leadership of equal competence and stature. There were faithful disciples, among whom was Jamasp(a) of the royal court, a loyal friend who succeeded Zoroaster as "pontiff" and whose son then succeeded him. But as the movement spread westward, eventually becoming in some form the religion of Achaemenian kings, the leadership passed increasingly into the hands of *athravans* (i.e., Iranian priests) who, though Zoroastrians by profession, were traditional enough to retain old beliefs and practices and to claim Zoroaster's sanction of them—even some he had clearly assailed!

The role of the Magi, the priestly class of Media, is obscure for this period. Nothing really can be inferred from the *Avesta* since it has but a single reference to them. We know, however, that it took some time for them to gain the trust of the Persian Achaemenids after the Medes had been overthrown. The probability, therefore, is that the identification of the Magi rather than athravans as the priests of later Zoroastrianism had its basis in the responsibility they took to speak for it during the Hellenistic period following Alexander's conquest (330-250 B.C.) when the Seleucids ruled. The question of what they did for the religion, however, cannot be clearly answered, either for that period or for the era that followed when native Iranian rule was restored and exercised by the Arsacid dynasty of Parthia (250 B.C.-A.D. 226). Zaehner may have been right in saying that the Arsacids "seem to have been totally indifferent to the religion of the Iranian Prophet,"[7] but that need not mean indifference to what Zoroastrianism *had become.* For that was the problem—what it had become. Though it was the dominant religion of the Parthian empire and there was an effort made by the royal court to recover and recall Avestan material lost and forgotten during the Seleucid era, such factors as political expediency, cultural and religious pluralism, and a cultus-minded priesthood spelled decadence for a religion which had no one actually faithful to the prophet to lead it.

Whatever, then, Zoroastrianism was at the end of the Achaemenian period, the religion that survived the conquests and rule of the Greeks and the Iranian Parthians could not have had either the pure inner substance or the influential patronage required to make it the people's principal source of spiritual succor.

At last, however, a high-born Persian claiming descent from the Achaemenids led a successful revolt against Parthian rule and inaugurated in A.D. 226 a new era for both the state and religion. Ardashir, founder of the Sasanian dynasty, was also—**if** tradition is right—of Magian lineage, and with religious zeal that had been lacking in even the late Achaemenids, he made his goal the revival of the religion and the establishment of the "Church" on a par, and in union, with the state. To this end, he instructed the high priest, Tansar, to reconstitute the *Avesta* (the body of authoritative Mazdayasnian teachings dating from Achaemenid times) from whatever fragments he could gather, both those memorized and transmitted orally by priests over the years and any written ones still extant.

The task was a formidable cne requiring an effort spread over the reign of Ardashir's successor, Shapur I, and into that of Shapur II who, when all the recoverable material had been collected, declared by edict that the canon was closed.[8] Meager as it was, it did provide the requisite clues for knowing enough about Zoroastrianism "before the fall" to effect a restoration.

The agents of the renaissance felt the urgency of the task along with its difficulties. During centuries of subjugation, the Persians could not have prevented the free circulation of a wide variety of

---

[7]Zaehner, *The Dawn and Twilight of Zoroastrianism, op. cit.,* p. 22 (hereafter cited as *Dawn and Twilight*).

[8]See Dhalla, *op. cit.,* p. 320.

religious and philosophical ideas even had they wanted to. Now, the architects of reconstruction found that the attraction of many of these ideas, and especially those of new dogmatists like the Manichees and Christians, posed a critical threat to the realization of their nationalistic ideal —i.e., a renaissance for Persia, defined in its politics by its own rulers and in its spiritual ideals by its own religion—for they might menace either the political or the religious basis of the state.

The priests and rulers of Persia were agreed upon the counter measures to be employed. Zoroastrian treatises (of the post-Sasanian 9th century) indicate that efforts were made to convert Christians inside Persia and whole populations of them in border territories, with special rewards and privileges offered as encouragement. However, if Jews and Christians on Zoroastrian home territory refused to convert, they were accused of following the "Evil Spirit," and Zoroastrians who adopted a rival religion were given the death sentence for apostasy.[9]

Apparently, strictures were only partially effective, inasmuch as there were Sasanians after Shapur II who had Christian wives and tolerance for the religion. But heretics within Zoroastrianism fared less well. Mani, the ascetic, spirit-matter dualist, gained such a following in the early Sasanian period that he was flayed to death (ca. A.D. 276-277). This served to discourage the movement in Persia, although its influence elsewhere continued for several centuries. Mazdak, of the early 6th century, was opposed because of his egalitarian social and economic doctrines. Anticipating that he would attract the masses, a zealous Sasanian put him to death along with most of his early followers.

Such measures, for all their effectiveness in some cases, were scarcely applicable when efforts by admittedly faithful Zoroastrians to reconstitute what they thought was good "catholic" Zoroastrian theology led to different interpretations. Consequently, there were unresolved sectarian conflicts throughout the Sasanian period. Suffice it to say here that some of them persisted as deviations even after the Muslim conquest; but with unity becoming crucial as an aid to survival, one main position emerged as dominant. It was the clear-cut dualism and mythologized theology found in the Pahlavi treatises of the 9th century.

[9]*Ibid.*, see pp. 325-329.

Post-Sasanian Times

The Muslims who conquered and succeeded the Zoroastrian Sasanians in A.D. 651 (652?) were Arabs. They had no need to oppress or persecute in order to win converts because the Zoroastrianism of the late Sasanian period was mainly form (ritualism) from which the spirit had all but vanished. There were, of course, staunch Zoroastrians who stubbornly resolved to preserve their tradition and found this the easier in areas away from beaten tracks. But then the Arab character of the domination was gradually diluted and "Persianized," and the policy of toleration for Zoroastrians was finally reversed by Persian Muslims. The Zoroastrian literary activity which produced the Pahlavi works ended with the 9th century when the climate changed, after which the faith's beleaguered defenders found survival possible in Iran only in the obscurity of isolated and economically-disadvantaged communities like Yazd or Kerman. Even there, repeated decimations reduced their number drastically so that by the late 19th century the Zoroastrians of Yazd numbered only 7,000 or 8,000. Kerman's survivors were fewer still—about 1,000. In India, however, wave after wave of them found acceptance as refugees during the next several centuries, to become there the advance troops of a resurgent Zoroastrianism.

Much of the history of the refugees—i.e., of the Parsis—between their first arrival in India and, say, the early 18th century is almost as obscure and fragmentary as that of their Iranian co-religionists. A favorite legend is that the Hindu rajah for the area where the first group is alleged to have landed expressed his fear of their overpopulating his territory. The leader of the pilgrim band is supposed to have replied that they would be like sugar in a potful of milk: they would sweeten it but not run it over. Tradition also has it that a 16-point statement of beliefs and practices was presented, so framed as to emphasize affinity with Hinduism and thereby win the rajah's permission to settle.[10]

The first fire-temple on Indian soil was built and consecrated a few years after the Parsis' arrival. It was an *Atash Behram*—the first and highest grade of Zoroastrian temples at which the ritual for

---

[10]Efforts to reconstruct the early history of the Parsis have resulted in positing several different dates for the arrival in India of the first group. They range from A.D. 716 at earliest to A.D. 936 at latest.

liturgical services is most elaborate.

With time the burgeoning community spread to four other main areas each of which, by the 13th century, had numerous parishes. Although the term for a parish was *panthak*, the group of parishes in each of the then five areas also came to be rather confusingly designated by the same term. The priests of each area panthak were then referred to, collectively, as *panths*, and each panth's priests, so far as is known, were of a single priestly-family lineage. When Muslims attacked Gujarat, the fire of the Atash Behram at Sanjan was removed and hidden, then moved several times more in the course of the next several centuries—once because of dispute between the priests of different panthaks. After 1742 when it was finally located permanently at Udvada, a part of the original Sanjan area, the Navsari panthak built a new Atash Behram, consecrating it in A.D. 1765.

The further expansion and concentration of Parsis in Maharashtra created the need for more ecclesiastical establishments. Between 1783 and 1897, four Atash Behrams were consecrated in Bombay, and two more were established in Gujarat at Surat. *Agiaries* (the Indian term usually used for temples with fires of the second grade, *Adaran*, and the few with fires only of third grade, *Dadgah*) are more numerous. Bombay today, with its 44, probably has more than half of those that have been established by the Parsis of India. The priests are not as readily counted as are the temples. Since the priesthood is hereditary, many priestly sons are ordained at the first of two levels (*Navar*) in order to have the privilege of performing the most frequently utilized rites, but only a fraction of these go on to higher ordination (*Martab*) or, for that matter, into regular priestly employment. Moulton estimated that there were about 750 practising priests in Bombay alone in the second decade of this century, but the great majority of these would be men "on call" to perform such services as time available from their secular occupations allowed them.[11] The number of priests is markedly less today, the percent of shrinkage much exceeding that of the Parsi population in general, which stands at about 85,000 for India as a whole.

Back in Iran two events of the late 19th century would finally improve the Zoroastrians' fortunes. In 1882, they were given

[11]James Hope Moulton, *The Treasure of the Magi* (London: Oxford University Press, 1917), p. 140.

equality with Muslims under Persian law. And in 1920 a new dynasty, with dislike for the oppressive aspects of Islamic hegemony, came to power in Tehran. Within 40 years, the number of Zoroastrians in the capital city increased from a few hundreds to about 10,000, while others were spreading again to communities they had once abandoned. The Kerman group of 1,000 had doubled, although Yazd, with about 5,000, had apparently contributed to the growth of the Zoroastrian communities of a few major cities. In all, however, the number of Zoroastrians in Iran has steadily increased, amounting in the late 1970's, as we have already noted, to approximately 30,000.[12]

The remainder of this chronicle must account for the rest of the world's Zoroastrians.

That there are Zoroastrians elsewhere is due almost wholly to the same ambition and industry that brought the Parsis to Bombay and to the prosperity they had achieved there by the end of the 19th century. There are of course some 5,000 Zoroastrians— almost all of them Parsis — in Pakistan, where they had gone as a part of their movement within India before partition. But the principal migrations have been undertaken by Parsis who, first as agents for the English and then as entrepreneurs themselves, found opportunities in other parts of the world for applying their enterprising spirit. Thus small communities began to develop in China as early as the 18th century, and today there are others—also small—in Ceylon, Burma, Singapore, and Japan. Further west, Aden at one time attracted as many as 750 of the faith, and slightly over a thousand have been among the Indians who have exchanged their sometimes bleak prospects at home for the opportunity to dominate business and trade in cities along the southeast coast of Africa.[13]

---

[12]See Mary Boyce, "Zoroastrianism," *Historia Religionum*, Vol. II, *Religions of the Present*, ed. C. Jouco Bleeker and Geo Widengren (Leiden: E.J. Brill, 1971), pp. 212-214 (hereafter cited as *HR II*), for statistics extending into the 1960's for Iran.

[13]Vimadalal, *What a Parsee Should Know, op. cit.*, p. 17. He may be regarded as a trustworthy reporter of the world Zoroastrian population in 1961, inasmuch as he had access to information held by the Parsi Panchayat of Bombay—the organization which Jamshed K. Pavri describes as the " 'defacto' mother-body of Parsis everywhere" and the one agency which has communication with "the various organizations spread all over the world " Pavri, who is Director of the Zoroastrian Society of British Columbia, and the writer of

In continental Europe, there are also upwards of 700 Parsis. But the larger communities now developing are to be found in the English speaking countries—especially England, Canada, and the United States where by 1973 there were about 5,000 Zoroastrians almost equally distributed among the three countries. In each country, the community seems to have increased by 100 per cent in little more than a decade.[14] The increases have derived, however, almost entirely from accelerated emigration from the older communities of Asia and Africa and not from a favorable birth rate.[15]

There have been only two fire-temples outside traditionally Zoroastrian areas—a Dadgah in Aden and one in Kenya.[16] However, Associations or Societies have been organized by virtually every one of the communities formed by migration. Several of these have priests serving full time but the others—including all the Western communities—are served, part-time, by priests in secular occupations. Of the communities without fire-temples, those of London and the Greater New York area are the only ones thus far that have established a surrogate—a *Setayashgah* (place of worship or house of prayer), although additional ones are in prospect.

Such is the story of a people defined by their fidelity to the Mazdayasnian religion, the religion of Zoroaster, the prophet of Iran. They may not always have been as wise as they have been faithful. As Zaehner has said, "Of all the great religions of the world Zoroastrianism was the least well served."[17] But they have faced with as much courage and bravery as any people the vicissitudes of their long history. While their continuing survival is presently a matter of grave concern, the way forward may yet be found by

---

a letter of June 30, 1973 in which the Panchayat was so characterized, also supplied data for bringing portions of Vimadalal's "census" of 1961 up to date. His statistics are corroborated by Cyrus P. Mehta, of the Zoroastrian Association of Europe (letter of May 5, 1973), and Dastur Dr. Framroze A. Bode, a retired high priest of Bombay residing part-time in Southern California (letter of May 14, 1973).

[14] The estimate is arrived at by comparing Vimadalal's figures for 1961 with those cited in the letters from Pavri and Mehta in 1973.

[15] On this point, all correspondents cited in n. 13 were agreed.

[16] Pavri, in letter cited.

[17] Zaehner, *op. cit.*, p. 170.

either the Iranians or the Parsis, or even, perhaps, by the newer communities. And the principle of *Shayest-ne-shayest*, permitting the bending of practice according to the prevailing circumstances, might be that way.

CHAPTER 2

Scriptures and Doctrines

We have now identified the Zoroastrians and those composing their largest single—and, in recent times, modestly dispersed—community, the Parsis. Meanwhile, little has been said about the substance of the faith which, after all, enough people having embraced it, sets Zoroastrians apart as a distinctive religious community. This substance, composed initially of the beliefs and convictions of the prophet Zoroaster but also of both older and later ideas added by his followers, found expression in Scripture, the *Avesta*, the composite work that became for subsequent generations the principal source of their inspiration, renewal, and regulation. We will look for the moment at the theology which has evolved from it, together with doctrines of man and his destiny, leaving for later the ideas that inform the cultus and define morality.

Zoroaster and his Gathas

The religion of Zoroaster before he sought its reformation was Indo-Iranian religion, a version of a body of religious beliefs that had been held by the large Indo-European multi-tribal community in general before various groupings within it migrated elsewhere—as to Iran—from the steppes of Asia. The early Vedic religion of those who went India-ward was a comparable modification of the older religion affected by a different experience. A significant central core of the older belief and practice, however, may be verified as having survived for a long time with but little change before Zoroaster undertook its criticism and revision in Iran.

Common to both Iranian and Indian versions of the earlier religion were numerous deities personifying the forces and vitalities of nature, their functions differing according to whether they were powers operating within the immediate environment and the human community or in the more distant reaches of the sky or cosmos. The name of a deity might change slightly and be different in Iran from what it was in India because of the evolution of languages, but many names remained the same. In any event, it is clear that it was customary in both traditions to classify the deities as either *ahuras* (the Vedic *asuras*) or *daevas* (the Vedic *devas*). Both classes apparently comprised deities benevolent and good as well as those malevolent and destructive.

How Zoroaster assayed that *Weltanschauung* (world view) is revealed in his Gathas. These are prayer-hymns he composed in poetic form to distill and enshrine, in language both memorable and memorizable, the record of his spiritual journey. Only five of them (comprised of 17 chapters in all) have survived, yet these suffice for reconstructing the main lines of his thought and the decisive events of his life.[1]

---

[1]The language of the Gathas we know only as Gathic because they are the only literature employing it that has been preserved. How many such hymns Zoroaster composed and were memorized by the priests of the Achaemenid period will never be known, for the five were all that were recalled or found when the Sasanids undertook the reconstruction of the *Avesta* in the original and for translation into the Pahlavi language. Even the five could be only imperfectly translated because Gathic had already become archaic before the priests supplemented the Gathas with their own compositions in Avestan—another language the name for which we are obliged again to borrow from the term denoting the literature itself, i.e., the *Avesta*. Progress has been made, in modern times, in decoding elements of the Gathas that baffled the Pahlavi translators; yet obscurities still remain. The translators were somewhat more successful with the Avestan language, inasmuch as it more nearly resembled both the Old Persian which supplanted it and their own Pahlavi or Middle Persian into which the Old Persian had evolved by Sasanian times.

It will be helpful at this point to list the divisions of the reconstructed *Avesta* —the present canon representing only about one-fourth of the 21 Books (*Nasks*) which are believed to have composed the *Avesta* of Achaemenid times:

1. The *Yasna*, of 72 chapters (*Has*), incorporating the 5 Gathas (17 of the chapters) and one later Gatha, the Gatha of the Seven Chapters (*Haptanghaiti*) that is not ascribed to Zoroaster. Prayers used in the worship of many deities, with some prominence given in the non-Gathic material to *Haoma*, the worship of whom was involved in all the many liturgical rites that included the use of the intoxicating or hallucinatory juice of the Haoma plant.

2. The *Visparad*, of 23 chapters (*Kardas*) supplementing the Yasna. Invocations to angels used especially at 6 seasonal festivals called *gahambars*.

3. The *Videvdat* (or, as often corrupted, *Vendidad*), of 22 chapters (*Fargards*), preserving the 21st and only completely salvaged Nask. A legal and

His theology is shown to have developed from the way in which he treated the traditional dual classification of the deities. Of the ahuras, we hear of only one *supreme* deity worthy of worship, Ahura (Lord). He then linked with that title another one, *Mazda* (Wisdom), a word already familiar in Iran. There may have been precedent for this association, but we do not know for sure. In any case, whether he used one or the other alone, or the two together— sometimes in one order and sometimes in reverse—he meant that there is only one who is really the supremely good God, Ahura Mazda. It may seem curious that nowhere (in the Gathas we possess) did he deny the existence of other ahuras, but he mentioned none by name; and it was to one deity only that he ascribed *all* positive attributes, thus marking his system as perhaps a henotheism or, alternatively, a qualified monotheism.

His treatment of the daevas was likewise and uniquely his own. He saw them as the deities worshipped by the lawless, marauding nomads of the society. Their wills were one—to do evil. The semi-settled, pastoral tribesmen should worship deity only of the ahura type. If they then attended in any way at all to the daevas as well, they might not be honoring or adoring the daevas, but they were implying respect for their powers by entreating and placating them with sacrifices in order to ward off the evil they could do. The word of Zoroaster to one and all was that to pay either type of heed to the daevas was false religion. They were not true gods; they were the Evil Spirit (*Angra Mainyu*) and the hosts of evil who had sprung from his Evil Mind (*Aka Manah*). They were not to be honored, even by placation; they were to be fought, relentlessly, and all

---

liturgical book, "against demons," consisting of regulations for avoiding, punishing, and atoning for evil, notably pollution. A work which Karl F. Geldner, in 1904, called "the Leviticus of the Parsis"—a phrase so apt that it has become common property by frequent usage.

4. The *Yashts*, 21 invocations to divinities of various ranks, but especially angels, for whom days of the month are named.

5. The *Khordeh Avesta*, or "Little Avesta," often combined with the Yashts in one manuscript, and intended for priests' and laymen's use or for services attended by laymen. Principal parts are prayers (*Nyaishes*) to address to the Sun, (*Mihr*, the light of the Sun), Moon, Water and Fire; prayers to the genii presiding over the five divisions (*Gahs*) of each day; invocations to the genii of the 30 days of the month (*Siroze*); "words of blessing" (*Afringans*) for several purposes but notably to honor the dead and their souls. The only part of the *Avesta* using *Pazand*, a special liturgical version of *Pahlavi*, as well as Avestan.

their evil intentions brought to naught.

The rest of Zoroaster's thought flows with reasonable consistency from these presuppositions. Ahura Mazda's Bounteous Spirit, *Spenta Mainyu,* is that aspect or "son" who is creative of life and the good in life. To say that this is God's Spirit is to affirm that his goodness or righteousness is his primary and all-encompassing attribute, with other qualities subsumed as further distinguishing traits. He is thus the eternal enemy of Angra Mainyu, the Evil Spirit. Whether, however, to regard Ahura Mazda and Spenta Mainyu as alternative terms for God or to think of Ahura Mazda as Spenta Mainyu's "creator" is a disputed question. Yasna 30:3 refers to two primordial "twin spirits," one of which would be Ahura Mazda (Spenta Mainyu) and the other, Angra Mainyu. This would be ethical, theological dualism. Yasna 47:3, on the other hand, by referring to Ahura Mazda as the good spirit's father, has led to the idea that Ahura Mazda created both spirits and gave them freedom of choice, after which one chose good and the other, evil.[2]

Associated with God are the attributes (or other entities) which Zoroaster in some measure personified and referred to as Good Mind (*Vohu Manah*), Truth or Righteousness (*Asha*), Good Power or the Kingdom of God (*Khshathra*), Right-Mindedness or Devo-

---

[2]Students of the religion, unable to agree on a resolution of the difference between such passages, are consequently also without agreement on what to call Zoroaster's theology. If he believed in only one Ahura Mazda with attributes, he was a monotheist (Zaehner's position in *Dawn and Twilight,* 50). If he believed that Ahura Mazda created other deities as aides, his system was essentially a polytheism or perhaps a henotheism (the term used by Boyce in "Zoroaster the Priest," *Bulletin of the School of Oriental and African Studies,* Vol. XXXIII, Part 1 (University of London 1970), text and footnote 83, p. 36 (hereafter cited as *BSOAS*) and in her *History of Zoroastrianism,* Vol. I, pp. 192-203.) But suppose that Yasna 30 : 3, with its reference to the twin spirits means exactly what it seems to mean; in that case, his system is an ethical, theological dualism. Simple dualism becomes a dualistic polytheism, however, if aides of spiritual nature are granted to each of the two protagonists. James W. Boyd and Donald A. Crosby in a sense combine two views. They find Zoroaster saying that when historical time began, there were already the two primordial spirits, but that in the course of their struggle, Ahura Mazda will prove to be the wise and powerful victor over the ignorant and artless Angra Mainyu. What began as a dualism will, when Angra Mainyu is annihilated, have become a monotheism! Boyd and Crosby, however, nowhere discuss the status of the Amesha Spentas or their opposite numbers. See their "Is Zoroastrianism Dualistic Or Monotheistic?" in JAAR, XLVII/4, (1979), 539-555.

tion (*Armaiti*), Wholeness or Perfection (*Haurvatat*), and Immortality (*Ameretat*). By right aspiration and obedience, man may participate in or conform his life to the first four of these qualities of God. The last two, Perfection and Immortality, cannot be won by man; they are bestowed by God as gifts to those who seek the other qualities. These six, together with the Bounteous Spirit, have been called since early post-Gathic times the Bountiful Immortals (*Amesha Spentas*). We know that the names of some of them were already familiar. But opinion is divided as to Zoroaster's precise intention. He may have been declaring that some familiar ahuras were actually only abstract attributes of God without separate existence. Equally plausible is the possibility that he meant merely to subordinate old ahuras to God by saying he was their creator and adding moral dimension to their character.

The ambiguity exists probably because Zoroaster's theological interest was subordinated to his preoccupation with the existential reality of evil, its threat to the quality of life, and the inescapability of struggle if evil was to be overcome by good. His theology, in its positive aspects, went little further than to provide a divine source and authority for his vision of the good life. The reality of evil demanded that there be a correlative postulate of a transcendent ground for it as well. The ground is Angra Mainyu, the Evil Spirit, who together with his Evil Mind (Aka Manah) and ally in wickedness, the Lie (*Druj*) do all in their power to subvert the righteous works of Spenta Mainyu, Vohu Manah, and Asha. Zoroaster's scheme of opposites, however, stops essentially right there, its incompleteness strongly suggesting that evangelism for the good life was more important to him than theological tidiness.

The concern Zoroaster had for man was grounded on the importance he understood him as having in the divine plan. Of all the creatures God placed in the world that he created, man alone is made to be God's ally. Thus, like the twin spirits of the spiritual realm, he possesses free will. If he chooses rightly and accepts his divinely intended role, he will conform his mind to that of Vohu Manah and his will to Asha. His rewards will be the gifts of wholeness (Haurvatat: well-being, health) and immortality (Ameretat). Everything that is the opposite of such boons will be his if he responds to the promptings of the Evil Spirit and his hosts, and becomes a participant with them in the battle they are waging at every level of God's spiritual and earthly creation.

Another chapter explains the specific duties of all persons who choose the good. Suffice it to say here that if these duties are accepted and the war against evil is fought bravely, Zoroaster envisaged a world made perfect in a final consummation, a final judgment that will bring an end to time and an eternal resolution of the conflict between good and evil. Zoroaster and his loyal followers will be entrusted with the perfecting of the world. Ahura Mazda, through (or supported by) Truth (Asha), Good Mind (Vohu Manah), and Devotion (Armaiti), will preside over the final resolution and judge the souls of men. The test is one of passing through fire and molten metal. Good men will pass through unscathed and even be purified by the ordeal but evil men will be unmasked and unmercifully seared. The lot of the good men will be eternal felicity with Ahura Mazda in his Kingdom of Righteousness, but for evil men, irrevocable doom.

The Theology of the Later Avesta

The Zoroastrianism of the Later Avesta is recognizable as having continuity with the Gathic picture of Zoroaster's reform. But there was change. Even if the substance of the religion was not so much altered as supplemented, this in itself wrought change in spirit or emphasis. The transition was effected in two stages.

The "Gatha of the Seven Chapters," a composition in Gathic prose that post-dates Zoroaster and reflects a change of situation for his reforming religion, represents the first stage of the transition. Zoroaster's reform, even if finally successful in eastern Iran, did not immediately establish itself in the west. If it was to survive among the variations on Indo-Iranian religion in the provinces, its voice could not be Zoroaster's zealously exclusive one but had to be the more tolerant one of accommodation.

The "Gatha of the Seven Chapters" (Yasna Haptanghaiti: Yasnas 35-41) and Yasna 42 indicate that the adjustment was made. Ahura Mazda retained his primacy but in association with other lords (ahuras), known by name and enjoying a marked degree of autonomy. His own nature as pure spirit was materially diluted by speaking of his having the sun for his body. A new genre of feminine powers (*gena*) rated notice as the waters of earth. Old Iranian religion's fravashis, the pre-existent prototypal souls of all men born and to be born on earth, were mentioned for the first time since Zoroaster passed them over in silence. And the concreteness of

Haoma was back. As a self-immolating god associated with sacrifice in the ancient cult, Haoma had been—and now was again—worshipped with intoxicating libations extracted from some plant and with the flesh of bulls or cows in ways which Zoroaster—without suppressing the cult altogether—had censured for profligacy. The teaching of Zoroaster was not forgotten, but much of the ancient religion he had so significantly reformed—in part, by ignoring it— was making a bid for re-affirmation.

The transition was completed by Zoroastrian athravans of the Achaemenid age. Their post-Gathic works, composing the so-called Later Avesta, tell us what they thought and practiced as "catholic Zoroastrianism."[3]

The several Avestan sections are not altogether representative of the same tendencies, but they are not contradictory—nor of such diversity as to prevent our making an economical summary of their general direction. Thus, the Yasna (the incorporated Gathas excepted) consists of invocations and miscellaneous prayers containing long lists of deities to be honored and whose aid or blessing was sought. As the text for a ritual that was in many respects pre-Zoroastrian, it had for a main purpose "the continuance, strengthening, and purifying of the material world of the good creation. . ." and "its daily performance . . . [was] essential."[4] Clearly, the implication is that every creation of God has been given a sacred vitality or life of its own and that it ebbs away or can be destroyed by evil if it is not ritually renewed day by day. This is not the same thing as regarding all that God has created as simply good and deserving of care and respect from man. On the contrary, it is the sacralization of material goods; they participate in sacredness because the "life" they possess flows into them from the deities whose function is their care and protection. But whence comes that vitality or potency which the deities have to spare? The answer seems obvious: from the offerings man makes as part of the rituals conducted by the priests. It can hardly be an accident that the six Bountiful Immortals (excluding the Bounteous Spirit) have feast-days honoring them,

---

[3]*Athravan* was the generic word for priest used in the Avestan texts. It was related to *atar*—i.e., fire, the veneration of which was a Pan-Iranian phenomenon. See Dhalla, *History*, p. 129. "Catholic Zoroastrianism" is Zaehner's term, *op. cit.*, p. 81. See pp. 79 ff. for explication of the difference between "catholic Zoroastrianism" and the prophet's "primitive Zoroastrianism."

[4]Boyce, *BSOAS*, XXXIII, I (1970), 24.

nor that one of them, Immortality, is offered fruit; and another, Good Mind, as the patron of cattle, is offered milk. Thus we come full cycle, the lesser deities (or the angels—*Yazatas*—if preferred; it is the same) invest the entities of the material world with their own life or vitality so that offerings of them can in turn be made to the deities for the renewing of their powers. Then the deities can renew every day the vitalities they had shared with material things in the first place.

That the Yasna alone is sufficient evidence for characterizing the late Avestan theology as polytheistic is not really in much dispute among present-day scholars. What is at issue is whether the Later Avesta was as much of a departure from primitive Zoroastrianism as an earlier generation of scholars supposed, and thus, also, whether Zoroaster was less of an ethical monotheist—or dualist – than they presumed. Suffice it to say that, historically, when polytheistic and ritualistic tendencies are in the ascendency in a religion, the definition of goodness and righteousness as cultic punctiliousness and correctness has also prospered at the expense of their definition as moral character and ethical conduct. Now, what Zoroaster is known to have said in the Gathas that did survive shows far more concern for condemning the ritual practices of which he disapproved than for prescribing those he approved, and far more concern for moral character and ethical conduct than for righteousness defined as the correct performance of a plethora of detailed and complex rituals. Again and again, he enjoined certain attitudes—right aspiration, right commitment, and discriminating wisdom—and not the mechanics of ritual as the marks of both acceptable worship and the moral life. There is therefore considerable plausibility for the presumption—and here it is better to speak of tendencies than of fixed positions—that Zoroaster tended toward ethical monotheism—or dualism—and the Later Avesta toward a ritualistic polytheism, in which case as regards both direction and spirit the two differed significantly.[5]

[5]Objectors to some part or all of this conclusion come from many quarters. Many Zoroastrians, stung by accusations that their religion is an outright polytheism, find the Gathas strictly monotheistic and are not satisfied with saying that Zoroaster "tended" toward monotheism. The priests, too—most of whom lack higher education in theology—have learned to affirm Zoroaster's monotheism; yet with few exceptions, they grant the Amesha Spentas and the Yazatas the status of subordinate deities—and this without any awareness of

The Visparad supplements the Yasna and only confirms its temper by lengthily "spinning out"[6]—as Geldner put it—the Yasna's liturgy for the six seasonal holidays (*Gahambars*) and their accompanying feasts. The Yashts, however, together with the Khordeh Avesta, dispel all doubt that the late Avestan religion differed from Zoroaster's, for there really seems no way of denying that the *Avesta* made his economy in theology a casualty of inflation. Unlike the Yasna where many divinities are addressed at once, the Yashts invoke them one at a time and capture our attention by the prominence they give to three ancient deities and to the fravashis.

Mithra, in the old Iranian religion, had been a junior, but essentially equal, partner of that ahura whom Zoroaster singled out as being light and truth and then exalted as the one Wise Lord, Ahura Mazda. But in the Gathas, he is not even mentioned. That is why attention is attracted by his reappearance in the Yashts as Ahura Mazda's creation or son, a deity upholding justice by insisting upon the sanctity of contract and treaty, and waging relentless war against all who invent lies or hold *him* in contempt. He was also understood as possessing the creating and preserving functions of the Bounteous Spirit (Spenta Mainyu), the theological consequence of which is the conflation of Ahura Mazda and his Bountiful Spirit (as in Yasna 30:3). Thus catholic Zoroastrianism supported the ethical dualism of opposing Angra Mainyu directly to Ahura Mazda.

The goddess *Anahita* was another familiar ahura of Indo-Iranian

------

contradiction

Zaehner and Boyce typify the marked difference there can be among scholars. Though Zaehner sees radical discontinuity between the "pure monotheism" of the prophet's Gathas and the unabashed polytheism of the Later Avesta, Boyce finds in both a fairly consistent "henotheism." The difference, for her, would be that Zoroaster's Gathic views are metaphysically the more exalted and his system of thought deepened by thorough-going ethicization.

It would seem that the "monotheists" may err in expecting the first real critic of an ancient polytheism to make the gigantic leap to pure monotheism all at once. At the same time, an argument such as that of Boyce distinctly underestimates the measure in which a prophet's lofty ideals are inevitably and necessarily made more concrete and common when less charismatic disciples fall heir to the task of making the faith succeed with the masses.

[6]Karl F. Geldner, "Avesta Literature," *Avesta, Pahlavi, and Ancient Persian Studies*, in honor of the late Shamo-ul-Ulama Dastur Peshotanji Sanjana, First Series, ed. by Karl J. Trubner and Otto Harassowitz (Strassburg, 1904), p. 8.

religion who, as "Lady of the Waters"—waters upon which the Iranian's dependence was measured by their scarcity—found her independent authority over water restored in the Yashts. She, too, received no mention in the Gathas of Zoroaster, the association of waters *there* having been with Wholeness (the Bountiful Immortal, Haurvatat) and thus with Ahura Mazda himself, whose gift they were as boon to man.

Verethraghna, as a god of war and victory, owed his recall from the limbo of Gathic silence to the place the Yashts give him as Mithra's agent in the war against violators of contracts and all enemies of the Good Mazdayasnian Religion in general. There is much that can be said about him, but it is enough for us to note that in being accommodated to Zoroastrianism, he was not shorn of the propensity for ruthlessness. His unhesitating destruction of enemies, which in the Yashts was made respectable, betokens a spirit at odds with that of Zoroaster, who sought first the conversion of his opponents and only after failing treated the unpersuaded as enemies and outcasts.[7]

Nothing in the Yashts having to do with the rehabilitation of some by-then half-starved gods, however, is as astounding as their recovery of functions that made even Ahura Mazda dependent upon them in the areas of their competence. The violence done to Zoroaster's theology was theoretically mitigated by crediting Ahura Mazda with the creation of the deities, but his divine supremacy was placed in jeopardy at the same time by the notion that in creating Mithra, in particular, he made him to be as worthy of veneration as he was himself. Ahura Mazda gave to him the task of protecting the whole material world as well as of vanquishing all daevic and human enemies. A house was built for him in heaven where even Ahura Mazda worships him. His portfolio bulged as he took on the assignments of protecting cattle, of granting men's pleas for sons, and of lighting the world by day after scourging the powers of evil through the night.[8] Anahita was less successful in accruing prerogatives, but it was she whom Ahura Mazda needed to persuade Zoroaster that he should adopt and preach the Good Religion,[9] and but for the fravashis, Ahura Mazda confessed that the human

[7] Yasna 44.
[8] See especially Yasht 10.
[9] Yasht 5.

race could not have survived or his creation have been defended against its total domination by the Lie.[10]

This is perhaps as much as we need to say to understand the main tendencies of Zoroastrianism from its rise with the prophet to its "time of troubles" that began with Alexander's victory over Persia. The monotheistic *direction* of Zoroaster's theology was seriously compromised by a return to popularity for gods obscured if not banished by his reform. This accommodation was achieved by ascribing their creation to Ahura Mazda and calling them yazatas (angels of various ranks including the Bountiful Immortals as a highest echelon of archangels). But the yazatas, for all of that, were *de facto* deities—cherished values and functions divinized and personified (or, if it be preferred, *re*-divinized and *re*-personified).[11] And one may speak all one wants to of catholic Zoroastrianism's retention of the Wise Lord's primacy in its theology,[12] but it was an empty honor if Ahura Mazda had to *ask* the help of his own spiritual creatures, even as having only one's title left was degrading to those Bountiful Immortals who found lesser angels absorbing their functions and then, as ranking gods, gaining ascendancy over them.[13]

---

[10]Yasht 13.

[11]We should add to those mentioned: Haoma, the plant-god, son of Ahura Mazda (Yasna 11), whose repeated immolation bestows immortality upon the worshippers of Mithra (Yasht 10, the hymn specifically honoring Haoma) so that he becomes, in effect, the usurper of the function of the Bountiful Immortal, Ameretat; Sraosha (the state of being obedient for Zoroaster) who in the later tradition is clearly a yazata type of deity rather confusedly conceived as both exercizing some of the same essential functions as Mithra (*e.g.*, routing evil and protecting good men on earth) and as exercizing these only *for* Mithra as his subordinate (Yashts 11, 12, and 10); Rashnu, another associate of Mithra whose functions overlap with his as confusedly as do those of Sraosha (Yasht 10).

[12]This is Boyce's tack when, in minimizing the difference between the religion of Zoroaster and that of the Later Avesta, she says, "All religious acts in Zoroastrianism are, however, first devoted to Ahura Mazda, whatever the dedication of the particular service [for which the *Avesta* provides the liturgical text]" (*BSOAS*, XXXIII, I [1970], p. 36). But pious genuflection can be made with or without a sense of actual dependence. There are other instances as well of Boyce's inattention to the necessity of having to distinguish, from time to time, between formal theory and what *de facto* practice indicates is functioning belief.

[13]As Moulton—who *did* distinguish, perhaps too puristically, between theory and practice—remarked, "The monotheistic theology is preserved, but it can

And yet, lest concern for theological tidiness be allowed to obscure the point and value of the changes wrought, it should be allowed that in all probability the willingness of Zoroaster's successors to try to be all things to all men may have saved the religion for posterity. It was a time, after all, not of reform-supporting Vishtaspas, but of Achaemenid kings whose interest in religion was in using it to justify their rule. A religion less eclectic and more capable of a critical stance toward both the social order and rival religious options might have marched straight into oblivion, taking both Zoroaster and his Gathas with it.

The Theology of the Sasanid and Post-Sasanid Era

The task of re-collecting and collating the fragments of the *Avesta* not entirely forgotten between 330 B.C. and the Sasanid restoration of indigenous Persian rule in the 3rd century A.D. was difficult only in a logistical sense. The more difficult problem was the theological one of deciding (*a*) what the reconstituted *Avesta* meant, and (*b*) whether the Avestan theology was adequate or due for re-interpretation and revision in order to render it defensible in an age of more intellectual ferment.

The ferment was the result of Persia's association with other cultures during the course of its rise, fall, and domination by others. Because of success as well as exigency, Iranian thought became aware of Greek philosophies, Judaism, and Christianity, and of sects intending to improve upon one or another, or all, of these major traditions. It is tempting, because it was at least a disputatious if not an exciting intellectual age, to describe and analyze these currents of thought in detail. But the temptation must be resisted, principally because our concern is with what went into the making of contemporary Zoroastrianism and not with what was discarded or fought off along the way. Manichaeanism and the Mazdakite heresy, as noted earlier, languished in Persia or died out completely after their leaders were martyred, the former surviving mainly as a threat to Christian orthodoxy in lands to the west. Zurvanism, a movement that attempted to counter theological dualism by making Zurvan, as Infinite Time, the father of both Ahura Mazda and Angra Mainyu, failed so completely that the Pahlavi tracts could be written

---

hardly be said that monotheistic religion remains" (*The Treasure of the Magi,* p. 100).

without making a single direct reference to the controversies Zurvanism had generated.

The religion then, that emerged as the result of the literary and theological efforts of an age extending from the 3rd through the 9th century A.D. (and probably into the 11th) had these several features:

1. The language in which it was couched was Pahlavi, a name for a dialect of Middle Persian that Zoroastrians used and that is therefore sometimes called Zoroastrian Middle Persian. The remnants of the *Avesta* as gathered together during the reigns of Sasanian kings were in the Gathic and Avestan dialects. The Pahlavi writers translated all of this material into their language, with the exception of some of the Yashts, and wrote their own tracts in which they described the content of much of the *Avesta* for which they had no remembered text. They also preserved in this way an enormous amount of myth and legend that had become the popular form of the religion of the pious and beleaguered faithful.

Names and terms employed during this period remained the same in the rituals because their texts were almost entirely from the *Avesta*. But in the tracts recounting and interpreting the history and theology of the tradition, the Pahlavi words were sufficiently different in many instances that confusion may be avoided if the more important ones are cited. Thus, Ohrmazd = Ahura Mazda, Spena Menu = Spenta Mainyu, Ahriman = Angra Mainyu, Amahraspands = Amesha Spentas, Yazads = Yazatas, and Zaratusht = Zarathushtra (Zoroaster).

2. The formal and finally dominant theological dualism was a reformed version of catholic Zoroastrianism. The old Iranian gods rehabilitated in the Later Avesta were again forced into retreat and regarded at most as spirits subservient to God. However, the coalescence of God and his Bounteous Spirit, implied in catholic Zoroastrianism, was reaffirmed, so that Ahriman remained directly opposed to Ohrmazd.[14] Neither of the two was without the trait

---

[14]For the dualist argument, Dhalla has pointed us to the Pahlavi tracts, chiefly the *Shikand Gumanik Vijar, Zatsparam, Dadistan-i Denik.* and *Bundahishn* (as translated in *Sacred Books of the East*). These agreed that God could not be father of both the Good Spirit and the Evil Spirit without becoming responsible for evil. Ahriman, then, had to be an independent being co-existent and at least temporally co-equal with Ohrmazd. In the end, of course, Ahriman would be vanquished and annihilated. These ideas explain why the Bounteous

of finitude, but the dualism was made at least provisional rather than permanent by believing in God's final triumph and Ahriman's defeat. The Yazads, including the Amahraspands (Bountiful Immortals), were given back functions they had lost to rival deities, but allowed a status no higher than that of created and subordinate angels.

This is not to say that exponents of a more monotheistic doctrine of God as the only creator—even of Ahriman— did not attempt to hold out against the dualists, but the Pahlavi tracts, by not even mentioning the minority position, make it clear that dualism became orthodoxy.

3. The dualistic dogma of the theologians, however, was not bread for the lay remnant of believers in Muslim Persia. Their sustenance was myth and legend, and this too, the Pahlavi tractarians were willing to preserve and magnify. Reference has been made earlier to old Indo-Iranian and Persian notions about the origins of the world and the prehistorical eras linking beginnings to the known and literate era of the Median and Persian empires. The *Avesta* refers, although but briefly, to these in passages of the legal section, the Videvdat, and also initiates the process of idealizing Zoroaster that ends in idolizing him. For the Later Avesta, he had been the first ideal man, the first to master God's law, and the one man on earth worthy—after his death—of homage in the form of prayers and sacrifices. But this was only the beginning. There are no religions that have not at some stage in their history mythologized one or more of their founders and prophets by identifying them primarily with a divine hierarchy, and by giving them the role of revealing to men the nature of the divine realm and how they may relate to it. Zoroastrianism is no exception. Fancy had had free play for five pre-Sasanid centuries when the task of preserving the religion had subordinated theological creativity. And the Pahlavi tractarians were as ready to pay court to these proliferating myths and legends in the corpus of the faith as they were to justify the religion with their dualistic theology.[15]

_____

Spirit was subsumed in Ohrmazd; there was no logical need for him in a theology that pitted the devil directly against God (Dhalla, *History*, pp. 384-397).

[15]An instance of expanding the mythological and legendary content of belief is a tract named for its author, *Arda Viraf*. It is a visionary's account of

There were three principal subjects upon which such imaginative thought expanded. The first was Zoroaster himself. His birth was foreordained, his conception miraculous and his delivery attended by archangels. Throughout his childhood and until he won final acceptance for his religion at Vishtaspa's court, repeated threats were made upon his life by demons and wicked men, but from all of these he was miraculously rescued.

A second subject upon which imagination played was the "cast" of the spiritual realm. On Ohrmazd's side, the Bounteous Immortals were valued less for their representation of abstract virtues than for their guardianship of six parts of creation.[16] We learn that each of them, as well as Ohrmazd, had three Yazads (Av. Yazatas—angels) as aides, some of whom—e.g., Mihr (Av. Mithra), Srosh (Av. Sraosha), and Rashn (Av. Rashnu)—had ranked as deities in the Later Avesta. Many were now named who before had been nameless—which did not in any way diminish the ranks of the un-named! Functions also changed in many instances and care for the living and their welfare in this world gave ground to concern that the faithful might fare well in the next world. The Frawahrs (Av. fravashis) were also re-conceived. Quantitatively, they were diminished in number, since only earthly creatures—and not every heavenly being as well, including even Ohrmazd, as in the Later Avesta—were thought to have such prototypal souls. But more obvious was an inconsistency that emerged in thinking about their nature. As some of the earliest creations of Ohrmazd, the Frawahrs were throught to descend to earth, each to become the soul of a new-born person. At death, the soul of the good and faithful man would return to its earlier heavenly abode, but descend for every feast day commemorated to the dead, to bless the living who honored it properly or to curse irrevocably those who did not. It is this conflation of the Frawahr and soul that introduced confusion. For dualistic ortho-

---

what he experienced in visiting both heaven and hell during a week-long trance.

[16]Man and animals, fire, metal, earth, water, and plants. See the "roster" of the Amesha Spentas, above, p. 16, with which this list of guardian functions may be aligned. It may be noted that *reference* to the Bounteous Spirit did not entirely disappear when dualistic theology made his position superfluous, but his functions became so much those of *Vohuman* (Av. Vohu Manah, Good Mind) that there was nothing he could do that Vohuman could not do just as well.

doxy, God's creations were good by nature, and it was not difficult to conflate the Frawahr with the soul of the person choosing to be good. But what of the case of the good Frawahr finding itself the soul of the person choosing evil? The conflation was then impossible, and the Frawahrs of evil men only could be considered, quite inconsistently, as "doubles" who leave their counterpart souls at the Bridge of Judgment and re-ascend to their appointed stations in the heavenly realm, while the evil souls go to hell until the final judgment and resurrection at the end of earthly time. In short, the confusion in the Pahlavi tracts consists in suggesting that the Frawahr and soul of a sinner are alike in essence but separable in nature, whereas the Frawahr of a good person becomes conceptually conflated with his soul. The consequence is that on feast days when an ancestor's presence and blessing are sought, only the Frawahr of a sinful ancestor can answer the call, but what is invoked in the case of a good ancestor can be either his Frawahr or his soul in the thought that they are one and the same anyway.[17]

So much for dualism's account of Ohrmazd's good spiritual creations. The other half of the story treats Ahriman and his evil ones. It is a half which has two parts. One deals with Ahriman's spiritual allies. Here again, we find the cast of characters imaginatively inflated. And—since reason is not a primary tool of theological construction when its task is preempted by fancy—the role pattern is far from tidy. The principal feature of the pattern, however, is that for every one of Ohrmazd's spiritual creatures, Ahriman conjured up an opposing demon of equivalent rank and power, each having its own mini-demons as aides and all of them together charged with tempting man to embrace every vice for which there could possibly be an opposing virtue.

The half of the myth that is Ahriman's story has as its other part what he did (and does) to God's world. He is described as not

<hr/>

[17]The confusion persists in the Parsi community although those who have become good students of their own religion have gone back to the Avestan view of the eternal distinction between fravashis and souls. This may clarify a point in theology but, as we will see later, the amount of attention ritually bestowed on both fravashis and souls at the time of death and thereafter for as long as the dead are held in memory has prompted reformers among those students to treat ancestor-worship as a pejorative term and to accuse the orthodox of perpetuating forms that render the religion of more use to the dead than to the living.

content to oppose and corrupt God's work, as in the Gathas, but as having balanced every good creation of God with an evil one of his own. Much of this is presaged in the Later Avesta (in both the Yashts and the Videvdat), but the Pahlavi literature was even more starkly dualistic; there, every difficulty met by man in the natural order—whether radical threat or mere inconvenience—owes its ontological existence to Ahriman. Thus, as just one example, the darkness which God gave to man as his time for sleep and renewal, but which could be misused by wrongdoers as cover for theft or murder, was transferred from the good to the evil order and understood to be evil not by its corruption in use but in it svery nature. Dualism, then, was not only one pair of ontological opposites— Ohrmazd *vs* Ahriman—but many: light *vs* darkness, truth *vs* falsehood, Zoroastrians who wear the identifying shirt and girdle *vs* those who do not, ritual purity *vs* pollution, life *vs* death, health *vs* disease, good creatures *vs* noxious creatures, life *vs* smoke, rain *vs* drought, summer *vs* winter, south *vs* north, and of course heaven *vs* hell.

The third subject upon which the imagination played in the Pahlavi period was the destiny of man and the eschatological future, including the epochs during which saviors appear, a final universal judgment, the glorious renovation of creation, and the nature of Best Existence (Paradise, for which the Pahlavi term was *Vahishta Ahu*). With this subject, as with that of the beginnings of things, soaring fancies did not encounter limits, for they dealt with drama directed from and ultimately played out on the stage of the spiritual realm, and there, where the mundane and limiting realities of this world did not apply, anything was possible. The Pahlavi tracts show that full advantage was taken of the freedom to speculate in an age when defensive Zoroastrians found tasteless sustenance in reason and restraint, because they needed, as compensation for earthly trials, the sweeter viands of their visionary paradise to come.

There could hardly have been a question asked for which imagination did not conjure up a detailed and specific answer. The reader intrigued by the curios of a credulous age can examine them for himself,[18] but the concrete materialization of the spiritual realm that was involved cannot be entirely passed over on that account. The

---

[18]See the Pahlavi works in English translation, in *Sacred Books of the East*, or Dhalla's organized description of their eschatology, *op. cit.*, pp. 407-433.

exact location of the Bridge of Judgment was cited. The anxieties of the soul of a deceased person during the three days that pass before the Bridge is reached were described. Angels ready at the Bridge to judge and then to condemn or aid were identified and named. The exact weight of good deeds as compared with that of evil deeds, which decided whether the soul's destiny was heaven or hell, was exactly determined; for those whose deeds were in exact balance, there was an intermediate place (*Hamistagan*) where the souls would wait without undue suffering until the day of resurrection. Hell (*Achishta Anghu*), it was averred, lay deep within the earth below the Bridge. The soul consigned to it went to one of four levels according to the amount of torture his degree of wickedness deserved, and the punishment was made to fit the crime. Heaven too had its four levels, and while each accorded its own degree of felicity, no soul's station afforded less bliss than that enjoyed by angels; and ambrosia, the angels' own food, was the food of all.

A rough sketch of the "choreography" for all this fateful dance of souls had been provided in the Later Avesta, especially by the Yashts and the Videvdat. The outline for the last Judgment and subsequent Renovation was there as well. The Pahlavists only filled it in by defining times, locating places, identifying old and many new members of the production crew, naming names, and describing the process by which evil souls as well as good ones would finally be gathered into God's perfected and everlasting Kingdom.

Zoroaster had spoken of himself and his followers—whether present or future is uncertain—as the saviors (*saoshyants*) who were God's agents in helping men make ready for a final consummation. The Later Avesta had named three successive saviors, only the last one of whom was cited as a direct descendant of Zoroaster and given Saoshyant as a name. It was he who would be born, in the "supernatural manner" of a "superman", to a "virgin" immaculately impregnated by seed of Zoroaster that had been preserved and "watched over by ninety-nine thousand nine hundred and ninety-nine Fravashis."[19]

---

[19]Dhalla, *op. cit.*, p. 289. Persons familiar with the Christian doctrine of Jesus' virgin birth, and inclined to regard it as original and unique, have this Zoroastrian doctrine—already several hundred years old when Jesus was born—to take account of. They will find it relevant to read available studies of the diffusion of ideas among Middle Eastern cultures during the centuries of first Persian and then Greek imperial rule.

Finally, there is the scenario elaborated by the Pahlavists, especially in the *Denkard* and the *Bundahishn* tracts. All three *soshyos* (Av. saoshyants), of whom the last is named *Soshyo* (or *Soshyans*) are to be immaculately conceived by virgins at intervals of a thousand years, to combat the evils of their respective periods and to move the good creation nearer to perfection than they found it. During each successive millennium, evil will lose some of its power and dominion until, finally, during a 57-year period of Soshyans' activity, perfection itself will be achieved—one token of which will be that men then living will need no material food, yet be vitally alive.[20]

The end will be near when all the dead are resurrected, given new material bodies, and re-judged in exact conformity with the judgments rendered when they died. A few persons will have been so evil that they crossed over into the demons' camp and will perish with them. Otherwise, the resurrected dead will join the then-living in passing through a flood of molten metal. This will be felt as an agonizing ordeal only by the wicked among the dead, but they have purgation of their sins and release from hell as compensation.

The seared world can now be renovated and made the eternal habitation for mankind. Families will be reunited, but there will no longer be birth or death. Those who died as adults will possess the vitalities of the age of 40, while whose who died as youths will remain as though they are but 15.[21] With the earth thus repopulated, the time will have come for a final confrontation with Ahriman. All his creations except darkness will be destroyed. He alone will survive in his own darkness, forever impotent, completely dissociated from the Kingdom of Ohrmazd. The world that Ahriman can no longer touch is Paradise, and all mankind will live by the

[20] A part of this doctrine is that Soshyans will have the aid of a number of remembered heroes of the faith. Given immortality for their bodies when they departed from the world, they will return to help in the restoration of the world to its original state of perfection. It is a notion which, as we will see, is important to Zoroastrians of the sect, Ilm-e-Khshnoom.

[21] The age of 15, in pre-modern Zoroastrian times, was the rough equivalent of 20 or 21 in our more literate and technological cultures—i.e., in terms of entry into vocation, marriage, and social responsibility. Knowing that it was the same, of course, throughout the Middle East should give students a clue to understanding why Muslims took over this same motif of ages for resurrected believers when they borrowed the schematic outline of Pahlavist Zoroastrian eschatology as a general framework for their own doctrines of the last judgement and the end of history.

spirit, needing neither material food nor drink.[22]

It would seem that the vision of last things grew the brighter as the light of theology faded. Texts dating from the 10th through the 14th centuries reveal the confusion engendered by a sectarianism that dualism did not wholly obliterate. But for the most part, they treat of ritual traditions and, like the later *Rivayats* that answered questions posed by the Parsis, say little about theology and then only by implication. One of Dhalla's sub-headings is apt: "Almost every vestige of Iranian scholarship perishes."[23] The case might be put differently. The more theological dualism was gilded with legend and myth, the more decisively the locus of the struggle between good and evil was shifted from the hearts and wills of men to an external arena where the antagonists were angelic and demonic forces and men were only partisans of the opposing teams. Religion, morally speaking, had become a spectator sport. Or, returning to Dhalla for an analogy, "The sacred fire, kindled by the holy prophet in the remote past, was still there, . . . [but] only smouldering in ashes upon the altar."[24]

Theology Today

The task of making sense of, and explaining to others, the structure and content of contemporary Zoroastrian theology is at once both difficult and easy. Difficult, because—unlike history which has after all happened and can be sifted again and again by its students until *some* measure of agreement can be reached as regards its essential lineaments—the present is the age of the living who take sides and whose thinking is or may be changing as the result of confrontations between parties (internal stimuli) or of either the desire or the necessity to come to terms with society, itself a changing thing (external forces). No analyst can ever be confident, therefore, that he has read aright all of his data, impressions, and suppositions, for all the parts that make up the picture his analysis is constructing may be shifting in place and importance as he works. Much

---

[22]For those who are curious to know if the great Renovation will occur in their lifetime, the answer is No! Moulton used the dating derived by E.W. West from the Pahlavi texts to place the first soshyant in the 4th century A.D. and the second in the 14th century. The date suggested for the third, Soshyans, is A.D. 2398 See Moulton, *op. cit.*, p. 105.

[23]Dhalla, *op. cit.*, p. 440.

[24]*Ibid.*, p. 445.

less, we might add, can the analyst be sure that he is excluding his own bias from his understanding and interpretation. For the wish to enforce custom or to effect change is hard to nullify when dealing with the malleable present—and more difficult to detect than historical revisionism.

Nonetheless, the task may also be easy, or at least—because the subject is Zoroastrianism—reasonably manageable. For while, as Boyce remarks, "the present position of Zoroastrianism is complex", as a religion it "is characterized by immense conservatism," so that "essentially and in details . . . the later religion is unchanged from that of ancient Iran."[25] Moulton, were he still living to follow up his first (and only) *on-site* study of Zoroastrianism, would surely have to add a fervent Amen. He would say, at the least, that essentially and in most details the religion has not changed since he studied it 60 years ago.[26]

We may start by appropriating Boyce's typology for assaying the theological spectrum, and hope that it will also be useful when we come to every other topic treated by subsequent chapters. She notes first—and not without reason, as we shall see—the orthodox group, together with those of Ilm-e-Khshnoom whose esoteric sectarian views are designed somewhat curiously to defend orthodoxy rather than challenge it. The second major group represents the reform movement. Besides these, there are the "nominal believers" whose beliefs are vague and imprecise but still inclusive of the notion that a few principal rites are efficacious in gaining the divine favor; and "finally, agnostics and atheists" who retain their Zoroastrian connection by blood if not religion and are given by their prior wish or permission, or their families', the last rites when they die.[27] Obviously, neither nominal believers nor non-believers have anything to contribute to theological discussion even if by their presence and numbers they represent factors of great importance for the

[25]Boyce, "Zoroastrianism," *HR* II, pp. 233 and 211.

[26]See Moulton, *op. cit.* It was one of the sources I put over for perusal until I completed my first visit of investigation. Despite the frankness of Moulton's bias—he was pejorative in treating Zoroastrianism and unabashedly apologetic as a Christian—I found his principal observations strikingly identical to my own. It seemed in fact, that either his book had been mistakenly pre-dated by more than 50 years or he had placed the religion in a time capsule before he left for me to discover intact and unchanged a half-century later.

[27]Boyce, "Zoroastrianism," *HR* II, pp. 233-234.

religion as a whole, especially as regards its present disposition and its potential for survival. This leaves the othodox and reform positions as the only ones to consider, *vis-a-vis* theology – though there are differences within each group which make it impossible to describe either one as neatly uniform.

Unfortunately, all too little clarity is gained by finding that there are only two groups, with or without sub-groups, whose views are at issue. The reason is that neither Zoroastrians in general nor the Parsis in particular have concerned themselves enough with theology *per se* to make the theological vocation attractive and compelling to the best minds of any recent generation. As both Moulton and Boyce have observed, although half a century apart, the community makes almost no provision for religious instruction or the systematic teaching of doctrine. Moulton, for his part, lamented that a deficiency in "the critical faculty" made the imminent appearance of theological genius quite unlikely, while Boyce points to the concern with "the practice of religion" as, by implication, so preoccupying that theology is inevitably given short shrift.[28] One way of saying this is that ritual practice—i.e., the cultus (Boyce's "practice of religion")— defines theology, and that it is not the other way around. But the cultus of Zoroastrianism is a composite construction from the early periods in the religion's development, the parts and rationales of which have never been made consistent and coherent by the ordering principles of a single theology. The theological enterprise is never, therefore, given a position of priority, but is used to explain or justify now-this, now-that ritual practice or its reform according to whichever of several hoary ideals the particular apologist chooses as his norm. The results for theology are chiefly obscurantism, contradictions, and a babble of tongues. But enough of reasons (or excuses) for postponing the attempt to say what is believed, however problematical that belief may prove to be.

As a preliminary remark, it may be said that most contemporary exponents of the tradition, whether orthodox or reformist, are in greater or lesser measure reverting to the *Avesta* and its two languages, Gathic and Avestan, for their vocabulary of essential

---

[28]See Moulton, *op. cit.*, pp. 171 and 173, and Boyce, *ibid.*, p. 230. A paucity of theologians, however, should not prompt the inference that there are no critical scholars among Zoroastrians of the modern period. But with regard to this, see my observations later in this chapter.

religious terms, and allowing the Pahlavi (Middle Persian) forms to fall gradually into disuse. There are at least two reasons for this. One is that, after all, the texts for the entire cultus are in the languages of the *Avesta*, the only exceptions being some short and supplementary benedictory prayers in Pazand, a post-Pahlavi dialect, and, similarly, the "sermonic" portions of such ceremonies as weddings. Surely it makes sense, if all the technical terms for theological discourse are drawn from languages already "dead" anyway, that economy should be effected by choosing the forms found in the languages they actually use for their treasured rituals. A second reason for this trend is more theological because it is related to a trend in theology *per se.* This is the trend that consists of looking backward to the original deposit of prophetic revelation and early development of the religion for "a pristine purity" not compromised or sullied by later accretions of inferior doctrine or by tendencies to re-mythologize the religion. Again, there is sense—if the most defensible foundations of the faith are, indeed, to be found in the earliest traditions—in supposing that they may be expounded more understandably if the technical terms used in their original expression are not exchanged for later and no less archaic derivations. Behind both of these reasons may be noted also the need felt by both orthodoxy and reform to counter with persuasive argument the criticism of non-Zoroastrian monotheists.

That having been said, however, the case seems to be that the reformers are the more purist than the orthodox in their effort to ground the religion in its "primitive truths." That is to say, reform is willing to prune away not only the imaginative excesses of the Pahlavi age but to question any portion of the Later Avesta found at odds with what Zoroaster said in his Gathas. Orthodoxy refuses to go that far because of all things that might be given up, the traditional cultus is not one of them. And since the Later Avesta provides most of the material for the liturgical texts as well as theological mandates for the rituals, the orthodox are perforce required to invest a great effort in interpretation of the Later Avesta in order to answer criticism from within and without. Then if the interpretation itself remains unconvincing, all that is left—for to concede more is unthinkable—is to fall back on tangential arguments for which they assume an *a priori* validity.

One such argument—already alluded to in the Introduction—is that age is a criterion for determining the truth-value of doctrine.

Reform has its own scattered exponents of this notion, but in returning to primitive Zoroastrianism, the majority is content to accept for Zoroaster the approximate dates suggested by historians uninterested in theological apologetics. If they employ the argument of age at all, it is the age of Zoroaster and not the Later Avesta that concerns them, and any of the 2nd or early 1st millennium suggestions is an early enough date to have such truth-value as age is alleged to guarantee. Orthodoxy, however, seems more united in its position, that of being determined to identify the age of Zoroaster as that of about 8,000 years ago. Some of its polemicists go further, asserting that authentic "Mazdayasnism—Mazda-worshipping religion—began several thousands of years before Zarathushtra." Thus there was truth before *his* time, and his mission was not that of a founder of a new religion or a reformer of age-old error, but one of restoring "pristine purity" to Mazdayasni religion by ridding it of "the evil of devayasni. . . ."[29] Another apologist is even more precise in his dating. "As per my humble research," he writes, "our revered Prophet was born on [the day of] *Roz Hormazd, Mah Fravardin . . . 6,325 years before Christ,* most probably at dawn." For him, the idea that there had been an earlier age of pure theological truth is reinforced by noting that science as well, "the art of the Magi Priests, had reached its zenith: [for in those days] people could fly in the air . . . [and] fire could be summoned to our kitchen as and when desired (electric installation), etc." The Golden Age, however, deteriorated because "the Scientists of those hoary days" were able to put their knowledge to evil use as well as good. They "could stop the rains at any time; destroy a whole city in minutes (atomic explosion), and so on." Together with "continuous wars and rumours of war and murder . . ." the evils of the age required the advent of Zoroaster if ancient truth was to be proclaimed afresh and men's feet turned once more toward the path of righteousness.[30]

[29]Ervad Dr. M. D. Karkhanavala, B.A., M.Sc., M.S., Ph.D., "Parsis, be true Mazdayasni-Zarathoshtis," in *Memorial Volume,* Golden Jubilee of the Memorial Column at Sanjan 1920-1971 and The Birth Centenary of Late Mr. Jehangirji Jamshedji Vimadalal, ed. N. E. Turel and Prof. K.C. Sheriar (Bombay: Bombay Zoroastrian Jashan Committee, 1971), p. 94.

[30]Behram D. Pithawala, "Era of Lord Zarathushtra—As deciphered from the letters in his Holy Name," *Memorial Volume, ibid.,* pp. 177-178. Internal evidence indicates the author's agreement with the esoteric beliefs of Ilm-e-Khshnoom.

This is clearly a rare instance of unfettered imagination, as is also, probably, the case of the reformist priest who is convinced that Zoroaster was predestined to be born on New Year's Day as a sign of the *cosmic* significance of his advent.

Such doubtful claims aside, the ardency with which all parties maintain their positions goes far to explain why the task of reducing orthodox theology to clear and succinct statement has its difficulties. Consider, as example, the orthodox objective of retaining all that *can be* by *some* means retained. This is not the *organizing* principle that would be provided by, say, the ideals of rational coherence and a more rigorously scientific historicity. It should occasion no surprise, therefore, if students of the religion find an obscurantism, however unintended, that permits of different understandings of what they read or are told. The opinion of Boyce, for example, is that the orthodox perpetuate the theological dualism of the Later Avesta and the Pahlavi tracts, according to which Angra Mainyu has his own independent existence.[31] But Dhalla who, given his strictures against traditionalism, can hardly be rated an orthodox apologist was clearly of different mind, when he wrote in the 1930s that "we hardly ever find even at this day *any* learned Parsi priest or layman marshalling arguments in vindication of the [theologically dualistic] doctrine."[32] (emphasis added.)

The contemporary work, *Zoroastrianism*,[33] written by Masani for English speaking non-Parsi readers, illustrates the problem one has in deciding what is thought by the orthodox who, so far, have retained their control of the institutions of their religion. It is Masani's contention that the religion is a monotheism because there is no spirit opposing Ahura Mazda that equals him in power. To be sure, there is evil in the world, but it is a principle not devised by Ahura Mazda; and thus to speak of Angra Mainyu as a spiritual being is merely metaphor. Yet Spenta Mainyu's existence as God's created and subordinate good Spirit is affirmed, along with the view that the Gathas say evil is opposed directly to Spenta Mainyu rather than Ahura Mazda. Thus when Masani needs to prove that Ahura Mazda is untainted by any connection with or responsibility for evil, he posits an *independent* (but otherwise

[31]See Boyce, "Zoroastrianism," *HR II*, p. 230.
[32]Dhalla, *op. cit.*, p. 489.
[33]Rustom Masani, *Zoroastrianism* (USA: The Macmillan Company, 1968).

unspecified) origin for evil as a *principle*. But when he wishes to establish Ahura Mazda's supremacy as proof that the religion is a monotheism in its theology, he appeals to Zoroaster, alleging that for him Angra Mainyu was the rebellious one of Ahura Mazda's Twin Spirits. There is also an unresolved discrepancy in Masani's explanations of the divine hierarchy. When he stresses the unity of God, he treats the Amesha Spentas and the Yazatas as his *attributes*, but when his purpose is to deny that there is worship of material fire and water, he says that only the *spirits* in such elements are worshipped.[31]

Current tracts published by orthodox authors for circulation among Parsis, and notes taken on interviews with orthodox priests, indicate that Masani has represented orthodoxy with reasonable fidelity. There is no budging from the claim that the religion is a monotheism, but beyond that—in accounting for evil and in defining Ahura Mazda's spiritual "creations"—there are no positions that all the orthodox accept. Nor does any one theorist seem to take a single internally consistent position. Thus Dabu has written that Angra Mainyu is "one of the twins created by God," "the destructive and ephemeral principle of Cosmos," "the destroyer . . . . [who] is not in revolt against God, but does unpleasant work assigned to him," the divinely appointed "agent . . . [who] is permitted to deceive and test all souls . . . causing death and destruction of form, until the world is ripe for immortality. . . ."[35] Satan would appear here to be the subverter of the "spirit and matter, Life and Form" that are the results of God's self-manifestation, yet Dabu says also that "wickedness is due to that part in man which we have derived during the evolutionary process from our material nature, and the body with an animal ancestry."[36] The difficulties are obvious. If life and form are divine manifestations, then material nature should not be, itself, the source of evil. But if having a material nature is the reason for

---

[31]*Ibid.*, pp. 48 and 64.

[35]Khurshed S. Dabu, *Message of Zarathushtra* (2nd ed.; Bombay: The New Book Co., Private Ltd., 1959), pp. 20-21. The author, from 1948 to 1977 the Dastur (High Priest) of Wadiaji Atesh-Beheram, Parsi Fire-Temple of Bombay, re-affirmed these theological views in an interview on November 19, 1971, when he was the eldest of Bombay's Parsi priests in active service.

[36]*Ibid.*, pp. 23-26.

men's wickedness, then is Satan needed as an agent? And if Satan
is doing work that God has assigned to him, how do we reconcile
that, on the one hand, with the idea that God is in no way responsible for evil, and on the other hand, with the notion that an agent
attempting to thwart God's will is nevertheless not really God's
adversary?

The two principal views among the orthodox about the Amesha
Spentas are that they are attributes (aspects) of God or his creations
with independent assigned functions, but there is little concern to
decide the matter one way or the other. There is more evident
certainty, however, that the Yazatas (angels) at the next lower level
of the spiritual hierarchy are individual spiritual entities who hear
and respond to the prayers addressed to them. The reason for the
greater certainty on this issue is not readily perceived. Perhaps it
is because the principal prayers of the liturgies are addressed to the
Yazatas and the one thing on which orthodoxy is unified is that
the traditional rituals must be preserved unchanged in order to be
efficacious. In any case, the orthodox are driven on that account
alone to regard the liturgical portions of the Later Avesta as having
a scriptural authority equal to that of the Gathas. They do not,
however, pay heed to the Pahlavists' imaginative multiplication of
the angelic and demonic personnel of the spiritual realm. With
respect also to doctrines about life after death and eschatology,
views are determined by the Avestan texts rather than the Pahlavi
tracts. Therefore, the only divinities associated with death and
affirmed in doctrine are four Yazatas that figure prominently in
the funeral liturgies, and while it is possible to find an occasional
believer in the Pahlavists' positive identification and dating of the
epochal saviors, the tendency is away from literalism. The "sons"
of Zoroaster, says Dabu, can be taken "in an allegorical sense" as
"more great messengers from God" for whom there is need "from
time to time"; and as for the end time, it "must be far away," for
"the universe does not progress with leaps and bounds . . . [but
only by] slow natural evolution . . . to bring about the destined
Utopia."[37]

The one group among the orthodox possessing a unique and
unifying ideology for defending traditionalism and its core of

---

[37]Dabu, *A Hand-Book of Information on Zoroastrianism* (Bombay: P.N. Mehta
Educational Trust, 1969), pp. 47-48 (hereafter cited as *Hand-Book*).

ritualism is a sect called Ilm-e-Khshnoom. Its lineage is not easily traced, but it appears to represent an effort to free Zoroastrianism from explicit alliance with late 19th century Theosophy by providing the religion with its own body of occult wisdom and esoteric interpretation of history and doctrine. Its interests resemble those also of an occult ascetic mysticism known to have attracted some Persian Zoroastrians in the post-Pahlavi era who were very probably influenced by Muslim mystics. Evidence is lacking, however, for direct descendancy on the part of Ilm-e-Khshnoom from this strain of mysticism, either doctrinally or institutionally.

The sect has virtually no structure of organization, but is constituted of the few priests and laymen who are willing to devote time to writing and to leading and attending discussion group meetings. The "master" to whose teaching these contemporary sectarians look for their Khshnoom (Enlightenment) was the late Behramshah Naoroji Shroff of Surat in Gujarat. He is alleged to have been taught the real truths of the religion during the 1870's in an Iranian mountain fastness where "Master-souls" and their followers had hid from the Muslim conquerors of the 7th century. There, from the chief master, he learned about the evolution of the cosmos, the temporal duration of which is supposed to span four great eons divided into 64 eras, each of 81,000 years; about Zoroaster's having known the truth because of his atunement to the music of the heavenly spheres and of how his followers had to translate his divine songs into earthly human language if ordinary people were to understand them; and how the preservers of the ancient lore are protected from unwanted discovery by an invisible talismanic barrier of miraculously repelling power.

Shroff is supposed to have remained in Iran only three and a half years (or until about 1880), when he returned to India to lead an exemplary Parsi life apparently conventional in all respects except one—he had been given a miraculous liquid that enabled him to turn copper into gold as insurance against having to pursue any occupation other than that of the savant. Yet he remained uncommunicative until about 1910 when he is said to have overcome a reluctance to share with others the secrets in his possession.[38]

[38]A confidant was Framroze Sorabji Chiniwalla, who attempted to explain the doctrine with exquisite confusion, in *Essential Origins of Zoroastrianism*, Some Glimpses of the Mazdayasni Zarathoshti Daen in its **Original Native**

A major objective of the sect is the reinterpretation of the rituals. Every artifact and action has a deeper hidden meaning than any provided by exoteric explanation. It is not enough to say that the consecrated urine of a pure white bull owes its current usage in purification rites to the fact that the urine of the cow "was believed by the ancient Zoroastrians to possess disinfecting properties,"[39] that feeding the temple fires with sandalwood stems from ancient regard for aromatic substances as symbols of divine power,[40] or that the sacred shirt (*sudreh*) worn by the initiated Zoroastrian has in addition to meanings for its separate parts the general value of being "a symbol that reminds one of purity of life and righteousness."[41] On the contrary, according to occult interpretation, "the liquid passed by cows and bulls alone possesses the special purifying property because the 'plexus,' the receptive centre (of magnetic current) operating on the urinary organs of cows and bulls is under the influence of Jupiter." Unconsecrated, the urine "remains pure for 72 hours from the time it is passed." But as *Nirang*—that is, as urine consecrated "through the elaborate holy ceremony of '*Nirang-din*,' [it] does not turn putrid for several years . . ." and so has the power when administered to the body every morning to counteract the "invisible microbes" that, in one's sleep, "envelop the human body and impair the *Khoreh* (aura)."[42] Similarly, the sandalwood becomes more than an analogical or metaphorical symbol. According to Chiniwalla, the greater the quantity of sandalwood that is burned, the greater the "manthric" activity of the fire upon which the very existence of our "Eternal and Temporary Universes" depends.[43] As for the sudreh, it shares with a girdle (*kusti*) in possessing "certain talismanic qualities which act . . . as a magical protective mechanism in times of crisis.[44]

The ultimate authority for this body of wisdom rests upon the knowledge that Zoroaster himself possessed it, for he was not a

---

Light of Khshnoom (Bombay: The Parsi Vegetarian and Temperance Society of Bombay, 1942).

[39]Jivanji Jamshedji Modi, *The Religious Ceremonies and Customs of the Parsees* (Bombay: British India Press, 1922), p. 67 (hereafter cited as *RCCP*).

[40]See *ibid.*, p. 321.

[41]*Ibid.*, p. 183.

[42]P.N. Tavaria, "Khshnoom: 'Nirang' ", *Parsiana*, April 1967, pp. 24-25.

[43]See Chiniwalla, *op. cit.*, pp. 224-225.

[44]Naigamwalla, *Zarathushtra's Glorious Faith, op. cit.*, p. 129.

mortal man but an angel—the deputy of the Yazad, Sraosha—
"sent to this world endowed with great powers and .... the
knowledge of all ages."[45] Moreover, it is maintained that all of
Zoroaster's revelations as translated into human language were
saved and hidden in a talismanically-protected place. Hence there
is a whole *Avesta* which only the "Master-souls" have known in
its entirety and which serves as the source for corrections and
additions to the fragmentary remnants known by the uninitiated
majority of Zoroastrians.

A principal objective that such speculation serves is, as already
stated, the defense of the whole cultus in as traditional and unmo-
dified a form as possible. If every rite, and every liturgical text for
every rite, are vehicles for invisible powers that illuminate, heal,
protect from harm, and eventually transform mortality into immortality, then tampering with any part of the cultus is obviously
unthinkable. Thus the sect serves to reinforce the orthodox theology of a pluralistic spiritual hierarchy as found in the liturgical
texts from the *Avesta*. Beyond that, however, the sect embraces
a doctrine of radical spirit-*vs*-matter dualism which the mainstream
tradition has always subordinated and given only minor place in
the total doctrinal system. That is to say, it is true that the
Videvdat discloses an ancient revulsion toward some aspects of the
material world—such as dead and decaying bodies, or creatures
that poison or threaten in some way other material creations useful
to man—and that much of this revulsion has not been dissipated
even in a scientifically more sophisticated age. But the doctrine is
that if matter is "noxious," it has been made so by corrupters either
demonic or human. Evil is therefore the consequence of devotion
to lies and of actions that are immoral. But matter, in essence, is
held to be the good creation of God whose intentions for it in the
divine scheme of things were wholly wise and pure. Correlatively,
the remedy for its corruption in the eschatological future is the

---

[45]Tavaria, "Khshnoom," *Parsiana*, February 1966, p. 25. The reader should
not be surprised to learn that Zoroaster's body was not a mortal one but "of
solid aura . . . lustrous and transparent." The corollary is that he could not
have been martyred by another mortal but was attacked by Satan himself
whose body he shattered. " . . . the Prophet's luminous body elements were
[then] dispersed and drawn back to their respective ethereal regions above
. . .," but such was the shock of the attack upon him that had he "allowed it
to strike against the earth, it (earth) would have been pulverized [sic]" (p. 26).

world's renovation—its renewal or return to an originally perfect state.

The praise reserved for the purely spiritual and the disparagement of any material embodiment reflect a sectarian doctrinal position metaphysically irreconcilable with that of the orthodox majority, however complete the agreement that exists on retention of the traditional cultus. Several of the sect's propositions make the distinction clear. Behind and above everything is *"Ahu*, the Absolute One in Oneness, the Supreme Deity over Ohrmazd and Ahriman."[46] From this One, a spiritual cosmos emanated, with various levels of spirituality for spiritual beings of different grades. Souls deficient in divine knowledge are relegated from the 8th and lowest heaven to the material planetary realm where the more recalcitrant of them become embodied according to "the *law of Infoldment of Spirit into Matter* . . ., [and] go through the *rounds of birth and death* . . . till Emancipation is gained . . . . [by the reverse process of] Unfoldment of Spirit from Matter. . . .[47] We hear of enlightenment for those who become adept in their responsiveness to spiritual vibrations, of pure matter being only fiery essence as contrasted with the concrete gross matter of our empirical experience, of immortality rather than resurrection or renewal, and the reunion of our "Divine Sparks" with the 'Divine Flame." This is none other than a philosophically monistic resolution of a dualism that is regarded as only apparent or provisional. When the process of manifestation, emanation, descent (of spirit into matter) ceases, then the reverse process of re-absorption begins. Its philosophical affinity is with Hindu Vedanta, but its fascination with mysteries makes it nearer kin to ancient astrological lore, Gnosticism, Jewish Cabala, and Theosophy.

There is little way of measuring the influence of occult doctrines such as those propounded by Ilm-e-Khshnoom. Many random impressions coalesce, however, to suggest that very few Parsis are theologically affected.[48] Nor are the few themselves particularly

---

[46]Tavaria, "Khshnoom: Numerological Expression," *Parsiana*, November 1966, p. 23.

[47]Tavaria,' 'Talismanic 81,000," *Parsiana*, May 1966, p. 25.

[48]Chiniwalla's work is now out of print, and *Parsi Avaz*, an eight-page Gujarati weekly devoted to propagating the cult, ceased publication in July 1974, its circulation having fallen from 3000 when it was founded in 1947 to 600 at the end. Whether the new bimonthly, *Dini Avaz*, launched in December

influential. If they are given a hearing by others, the reason is not credibility of doctrine but appreciation on the part of the orthodox for support of cultic traditionalism.

Any other sectarian divisions among Zoroastrians are based upon different calendars and comment upon them may be left to the chapter on the cultus. If there is any correlation between the calendar issue and metaphysics or theology, it is provided more by coincidence than design. That is to say, the same Parsis who believe in accommodating the ecclesiastical calendar to a contemporary secular one are likely to be reformers by temperament and thus ready to discuss new trends of thought in any area of religious thought.

As for reformers in general, they constitute a movement and are not identified as a sect. The priests among them are few, largely because most priests have an understandably vested interest in preserving the social and professional prerogatives which traditionalism underwrites. The reformers are therefore mainly laymen divided—how unevenly no one knows—between those who are aggressive and articulate and those who, finding that reformist agitation arouses only discussion but not change, settle for perfunctory observance of a few obligations that sustain their nominal membership in the Parsi community.

We have already noted that systematic theology is not a major interest of Parsis, but that they attend to it if and when they feel the need of disavowing polytheism. In this respect, reformers and most of the orthodox are similar, as they are also in making essentially non-theological issues their principal concerns. But when they do undertake to "do theology," they differ in that the reformers are the more radical of the two parties in their reductionism. The orthodox, professing monotheism, are prepared to repudiate the theological dualism and mythopoeic excesses of Sasanian orthodoxy, but they have trouble—as we have seen—in handling the theological implications of the Later Avesta because it provides the liturgies for a sacrosanct cultus. There are some who

---

1975, will attract its predecessor's lost subscribers remains to be seen. As re *Parsi Avaz*, see Pervin Mahoney, "The Sound of Silence," *Parsiana*, June-July 1974, p. 23; and for a brief account of the new publication and the interest in new classes, Sanober Marker, "Dini Avaz," *Parsiana*, February 1976, p. 31.

do re-interpret the divinities to whom prayers are addressed, by denying the need to be literal and saying that the divinities merely symbolize the attributes and powers of one God. But for many, the lack of training in theology makes a venture into speculative thinking too hazardous to contemplate. The result is a re-affirmation of the literal existence of the divinities combined with insistence that their monotheism is not thereby qualified because one God created them and made them his subordinates.

The reformers are more reductionist because they are ready to reform the cultus and on that account find it unnecessary to defend the Later Avesta as authoritative for contemporary Zoroastrianism. Their common maxim is "Back to the Gathas." This modern impulse thus to go back to "primitive" Zoroastrianism is probably to be associated with the founding in 1851 of the *Rahnumae Maz-dayasnan Sabha*, a society that has sought "to dissuade Parsis from superstitious and un-Zoroastrian beliefs and to present to them the teachings of the Prophet Zarathushtra in their original and pure form."[49] Further impetus was given to reform when the K.R. Cama Oriental Institute was founded in Bombay in 1916. While the Institute's objective was not reform but the promotion of scholary inquiry, the results have certainly aided the cause of reform by indirection—that is, by supplying reformers with knowledge of how Zoroastrian traditions in particular evolved and with criteria for distinguishing between their historical and mythopoeic elements. Today, neither the Sabha nor the Institute (where, since its founding, the Sabha has centered its educational activities) serves as a vigorous generator of reformist sentiment, but their legacy has been the diffusion of such sentiment among many individual members of the Parsi community.

The theological element of this legacy is characterized by what has become a basic aim of reform: the establishment of the claim that Zoroaster's own theology—and the theology that should therefore be normative—was a clear-cut monotheism. The first corollary is that the Gathas are *the* authoritative Scripture, so that all Later Avestan writings have their value determined by whether they accord with or depart from Gathic conceptions. A second corollary is that any doubt allowed by the Gathas as to whether the

---

[49]Jehangir M. Ranina, "We Parsis," *Parsiana*, February 1969, p. 7.

Bounteous Spirit and the Bountiful Immortals are attributes of God or other divinities he has created is resolved by insisting that they are the former—as Dhalla says, "pure abstractions, ethere-alized _moral concepts, symbolic ideals, abstract figures."[50] As God's attributes and states of perfection, they constitute the ideals after which man should pattern his own life in order that he may be worthy of God's benefactions and of admission to the "Abode of good mind," the "House of Song," the Kingdom of God.

The avoidance of polytheism or theological dualism is not com-plete, however, until it is shown that Angra Mainyu as well is not a spirit of God's creation or a rival deity. The reform position taken by many is that the evil one of the "Twin Spirits" is to be understood as a simple admission of the fact that evil must exist since men choose it. There does seem to be no question but that the Gathas posit human freedom and regard righteousness as an empty concept unless man makes it his ideal or way of life *by choice*. It then follows by logical necessity that man may choose its opposite. And if that is so, then God did not create a separate spirit and give him an evil nature, or foreordain his choice to be evil; rather, he allowed the possibility of evil as the condition of there being any meaning for goodness. There is no cosmic spiritual entity that is Angra Mainyu. "He" is simply the spirit in which people act who live by lies, violence, and wrath. According to one reformer, the Devil and his hosts were, for Zoroaster, the priests of his time who "put the fear of the Devil and demons in men and induced them into ceremonies to scare these away."[51] Dastur Bode sees Zoroaster as solving the problem of evil by declaring that "evil is not an entity or a being: it is only the twin mentality and relativity in the human mind."[52]

[50]Dhalla, *op. cit.*, p. 39.

[51]Dara J.D. Cama, *We Parsis, Our Prophet, and Our Priests* (Bombay, 1966), p. 11. Cama, a Bombay real estate agent, is a lay reformer more sharp-tongued than most in his criticism of traditionalism.

[52]Framroze A. Bode, "Religion and Modern Man," a Reprint from *Dipanjali*, June 1967, New Delhi, p. 4 (of reprint). Dastur Bode, one of the few reformist priests of Bombay at midcentury, has in recent years lived part-time in California, lecturing and performing outer ceremonies there as in Bombay. Although as sympathetic to Vedanta as Dastur Dabu to Theosophy, his interest lies in relating the religion adaptively to contemporary need, whereas Dabu emphasizes mainly the importance of preserving traditions intact.

One area of doctrine about which reformers say very little is that of eschatology. One may infer that the speculative imagination is not kindled by hope of a future kingdom of righteousness if the prospect is that there will be no then-living Zoroastrians to aid in its inauguration. Lay reformers are preoccupied with trying to initiate change in traditional practices which they believe are the causes of the community's declining numbers. This leaves theological reflection to the priests among whom there are but a few of reform temper. Among these few, Dastur Bode is probably the most published spokesman, and he spares but a few paragraphs for eschatology in writings otherwise devoted to commending Zoroastrianism as a religion for modern man. His vision is one of a final judgment, the annihilation of all evil by ordeal, and a new everlasting heaven and earth. "Zarathushtra's message," he writes in succinct condensation of his eschatological doctrine, "is full of hope, optimism and cheer; the ultimate triumph of good and transmutation of evil into good are assured."[53]

Until that time, the reform view of human destiny is that the souls of the deceased may be safely left to the mercies of God who, if good, is also just. No demons need be frightened away or angels implored to guarantee safe passage of departed souls to the bar of judgment. That being the case, the polytheism of the funeral liturgies can be declared archaic and the rites be understood as having only the functions of honoring the dead and comforting the mourners.

Zoroastrian doctrine is obviously not one systematized and generally approved body of theological and philosophical tenets but several sets of tenets for each of which the claim is made that it represents early and therefore normative Zoroastrianism. "Early," in its turn, can mean either Zoroaster's Gathic doctrines or the doctrines of the whole *Avesta*. Lack of agreement, however, is not necessarily ennervating. A religion *can* be the more vital the more vigorously its ideological bases are debated. The problem is that the community lacks the leadership able by training or motivated by desire (1) to winnow appealing and viable theological insights from the chaff of many accretions, (2) to explain and interpret the salvaged insights for successive generations, and (3) to submit the insights repeatedly to the tests which knowledge acquired from any

[53]*Ibid.*

quarter may pose.

The present situation is that there are the priests trained mainly in the proper conduct of ritual and recitation of the liturgical texts. They are unprepared to engage in theological construction. Then there are the scholars, some of them priests and others laymen, who have pursued studies in history, philology and philosophy. They have the tools requisite for advanced theological reflection, but few if any are willing to enter the arena of debate where they would be distracted and diverted from objective research. Unfortunately, the few who are willing seem unaware of their need to engage, additionally, in comparative, phenomenological, and sociological studies of religion if they aspire to become credible apologists rather than educated partisans. A narrow-gauge education, however "advanced," cannot provide the perspectives necessary to appreciate Zoroaster's existential situation. Like all great prophets, Zoroaster was dealing with an immediate and preoccupying crisis. To do so decisively and successfully required addressing himself only to the questions and issues it involved and to answering only the questions thus raised. The task of fitting any prophet's thought into a total *Weltanschauung* that itself might have to be restructured to accommodate the new prophetic insight has always devolved upon his followers. This was the case with Zoroaster but it has not been understood by his followers, with the consequence that they impute to him one or another set of final answers to ultimate ontological questions when his one overriding concern was the moral crisis of his time. By then proceeding to regard their respective versions of his allegedly "total" system as eternally valid and immutable, they cut the nerve of that fresh inquiry which alone would bespeak fidelity to the prophet's spirit.

The climate of the last quarter of the century is thus not significantly different from that of half a century ago when Moulton found the Parsis anxious to preserve understanding of the aims and symbolism of their ceremonies but given to "credulity at one end, almost complete denial at the other . . ."[54] as regards systematic theology. Believers themselves are not lacking awareness of need for a fresh burst of theological creativity, but rites and customs are their overriding concerns in the 20th century. The same can be said of the Iranis and Westerners, though there is a difference. Those

[54]Moulton, *op. cit.*, p. 170.

outside of India are having perforce to make their first order of business that of meeting the challenge of adjusting their practices and making them functional within societies which they have had no share (or early share) in shaping. They are meeting this challenge willingly and with reasonable concord. It may be their youth who, when the task is well along, may turn to the long-languishing discipline of theology and effect its renewal. The Parsis have their own way of responding to the pressures exerted by their more familiar but nevertheless changing society. It is to talk and wait, and wait and talk—which, because it is a way that postpones action also prevents moving on to other business. One would guess that it is not to the Parsis, therefore, that the new theologians are likely in any immediate future to be born.

CHAPTER 3

The Institutional Structure

Institutions may be established habits or actions, corporate organizations, or—by association with organizations—even the buildings or facilities that come into use as the place for actions organizationally sponsored. Three of Zoroastrianism's oldest institutions represent the kinds allowed by this definition: the veneration of fire, the priesthood, and the fire-temples.

Both the priesthood and the ritual use of fire antedated the temples. It has already been noted that an Iranian priesthood as a class of ritual functionaries existed well before Zoroaster's time. He himself may have been trained as a priest, but as a prophet too, he aimed at the reform of what he had been taught. In other words, the Zoroastrian priesthood was not a new order that he instituted but an existing class some of whose members he had to win if reform was to be effected.

Fire-Temples and Their Governance

One feature of the reform, authorities agree, was Zoroaster's special emphasis on fire as symbol *par excellence* of his supreme deity, Ahura Mazda. Tradition cited by Jackson make reference to at least ten locations in pre-Zoroastrian Iran where sacred fires were kept burning, and to Zoroaster's concern for their care and increase.[1] It appears that the fires had been kindled originally in the open, on pyres built atop mountains or promontories, but that temple-building was eventually instituted as a protective measure against the exigencies of weather that could quench the fires. Some of the fires on sites associated with events or persons of religious import and which had burned without interruption for a long time

[1]Jackson, *Zoroaster, The Prophet of Ancient Iran*, pp. 98f.

are known to have acquired special sanctity. The principal thrust of Zoroaster's reformation, in this connection, however, was toward multiplication of shrines where freshly kindled fires would never be threatened by extinction. In this, Zoroaster was both logical and practical. If there was one supreme God whose existence was eternal, the symbol most representative of Him should itself, once kindled, be preserved in perpetuity. Besides, if by this visible symbol the religion of Zoroaster could most practically be commended to laity and their fidelity given support by their sharing the responsibility of the fires' preservation, then it was merely common sense to establish a fire and to house it in some way in every community where his teaching gained acceptance. Adapting the "cult of the domestic fire," thought by Duchesne-Guillemin to be another already developed tradition,[2] served further to reinforce Mazdean commitment by making the morning re-kindling of the embers on the domestic hearth an act of daily devotion to Ahura Mazda.

There is no need to say more about the sacred fire as an institution when its character and tending make explanation of it within the rubric of the cultus more appropriate. Reference to it, however, is necessitated because its centrality in the cultus has made it also the single most determining factor in shaping the institutions of the temple and the priesthood.

In the case of the temple, this means that its physical structure as well as all the uses to which it is put have been determined by its primary function, providing sanctuary for the sacred fire. The Zoroastrian sanctuary in early times and in the small villages was usually a portion or annex of the priest's home, the cost of which was met by the donations made for the performance of rituals attended or requested by *behdins* (the laity). A fire-temple, as a structure altogether separate and representing a later development, could be afforded if the community was large or if it was provided as a benefaction by someone of means or with access to a governmental treasury. As long as the worshipers were Mazdayasnian or already fire-reverencing, structural form needed to provide for little more than demarcation of the holy ritual area, where only priests were allowed, to separate it from the profane precinct open to the

[2]Jacques Duchesne-Guillemin, *Symbols and Values in Zoroastrianism*, Vol. 15 of *Religious Perspectives*, ed. Ruth Nanda Anshen (New York : Harper and Row, 1966), pp. 66f.

lay worshipers. The evolution of greater complexity of form is obscure, although the factors of significance for it are easily discerned. The eventual hegemony of the Magi was a victory for the mutually re-inforcing factors of hereditary priestly vocation and their penchant for creeping sacerdotalism. The consequences, which cannot be dated as to times of origin but which were clearly already traditions when the Parsis left Persia for India, were at least these: separation of the sacred fires into three grades, the higher first and second of which could be approached only by the priests; stricter separation of holy from profane areas by raising a latticed wall between the first or second grade fire and the lay worshipers; and addition of a room or hall for a third grade (lowest grade) fire which the laity (in the absence of a priest) might feed without profaning it. At some time, the incidence of non-Mazdayasnians in the country conjoined with the priests' sacerdotal concern for ritual purity to dictate a form for the temple that would prevent a *juddin's* seeing the fire from outside, for he was considered unclean and even his gaze would be contaminating. The result is a form, long since made normative for the Parsis especially, of having an outer hall as locus of entry and purification for the behdin, and an inner hall with a metal-latticed or glass-enclosed area for the *afargan* (censer: urn) with its fire.

In Iran where juddins are not excluded from most of the fire-temples, a wall enclosing the temple compound is enough to suggest sacred isolation for the fire inside the temple. The special entry hall is omitted, so that the enclosure for the fire, and the fire itself, are visible upon entering.

Inasmuch as no temple fire once consecrated may be allowed to die and the first and second grades in particular must be fed at the beginning of each of five periods (gahs) of every 24 hours, and since, further, preliminary rites of purification and recitation of liturgies appropriate to each gah are required, it follows that most temples have a collegiate priesthood to perform these duties which even when arranged according to shifts require a principal portion of each priest's time. The behdins, incidentally, play no active part in these ceremonies and may rarely attend them. There are, to be sure, some "inner" liturgical services held daily and on festival days at which the attendance of behdins is desired, but they attend at and for whatever time they find individually convenient and rarely as a corporate congregation worshiping for a set time. The few services intentionally congregational in type—the so-called "outer" ceremonies—are brief and usually performed either in a hall or pavilion near a fire-temple or in private homes in the presence of a third grade or domestic fire. A group of the laity may usually attend these, but it would diminish the meaning of the word to call it a congregation.

The point, if it is not by now clear, is that whatever the ways provided for the religion to serve the good of persons, the physical structure of temples is determined by the need to honor and preserve the sacred fire.

The organizational structure of temples is consistent with the physical. The pattern is based on philanthropy, not on membership. The temple is normally a benefaction established by a person of means, who usually provides also a trust fund for some measure of continuing support. The terms of the trust define the nature, structure, and membership of the self-perpetuating board of governance or, in a few instances, lodge authority with the local Panchayat or *Anjuman*. In any case, the managerial board's two main functions are those of overall business management and appointment of priests. This leaves the priests as virtually unassailable authorities in the areas of theology, ritual, morality and ethics. The people whom they serve are an informal constituency but they are not "temple members." They frequent the temple of their immediate community by tradition and convenience yet perhaps not even then if they are not too distant from another temple to which they feel drawn by old family ties or preference for its encumbent priests.

The Priesthood

The principle of occupation by heredity has been variously applied in Iran and Zoroastrianism. Only among the Medes do the authorities think the priesthood was hereditary in pre-Persian (pre-Achaemenid) times. Provincial rulers also had discovered the advantages of the hereditary principle. The society as a whole, however, was not yet of a complexity requiring great division of labor, and a person simply tended to do what his parents taught him.

The development of a vastly more complicated society was a corollary of bringing rival provinces together in a nation state, and of going on from that to create an empire. By that time, the four main classes were constituted of the governing bureaucracy and an elite military establishment, the priesthood, the rural population, and a business, commercial, and artisan class. Although in the interest of internal peace and security, all classes and occupations were made hereditary—a system which after the centuries of Iranian subjection to conquerors was re-introduced by the first Sasanian, Ardashir—the Sasanian application of it was liberalized and a person "by special qualifications" could "qualify himself for a profession, other than that of his forefathers."[3] After the Muslims' conquest, however, the notion of even a hereditary *ruling* class of Zoroastrians evaporated, and for at least as long as the Parsis can remember, the three non-priestly classes have been a single class without restraint upon choice or mobility. The priestly class alone has been hereditary in India, with no allowance for acceptance of any aspiring layman into the ranks.

Adoption of the priestly vocation, however, is not a requirement for those who inherit the right to it. Doubtless, the profession was one of prestige among the Parsi refugees in their early centuries of residence in Gujarat. This does not mean that all the sons of a priest automatically followed their father's vocation—so many could not possibly have been supported by communities whose means were modest at best—but as long as a priestly family had male descendants and a male of every fourth generation entered the priesthood, the general rule was that this sufficed to preserve the family's membership in the class.[4] Yet changing fortunes have brought modification to even so elastic a rule. Migration to Bombay opened up manifold opportunities for social advancement and for economic gain with which most priestly emolument has not compared. The number of priestly sons who elected secular occupations predictably multiplied. They could, of course, (and still can) train for the Navar ordination which qualifies them to be *ervads.* Some do this not because they choose it but because the ordination commonly occurs during the early adolescent years at the will of the parents. Ervads may perform the outer liturgical ceremonies and, for such occasions, wear the white turban, since present practice permits—as it once did not—alternating the white turban with a layman's black one by those

---

[3]J.J. Modi, *RCCP*, p. 198. Modi has cited a tradition to the effect that a famous Dastur of a time as late as the 17th century had "sprung from the laity " *Ibid.*

[4]*Ibid.*, p. 199.

whose lives are spent mainly in secular pursuits.

Yet, of late, the desire that sons take the first ordination has been in steady decline, and of those that are so ordained, many do not study for the second, higher ordination, Martab, and become fully qualified *mobeds*. On this account, there is, as all contemporary analysts of Zoroastrian "crises" agree, a shortage of ordinees making the priesthood their profession. It is understandable, therefore, why there is no longer an interest in requiring a family to be represented in the priestly profession by at least one male in every four generations if it wishes to retain its priestly class status.[5] The number of families that would leave the class and become behdins would further lessen the potential supply of future priests—a prospect apparently more bleak than that of honoring a tradition almost entirely in the breach.[6]

The Role and Training of Priests

To know the purpose and structural plans of fire-temples is to know a principal function of priests. Those who serve as members of a collegial temple staff must take their turns at feeding the sacred fire and reciting the offices of the associated ceremonies. Beyond that, they are called upon for performance of the outer liturgical services desired by the temple's patrons, but the demands made on time by the higher ceremonies, combined with a declining number of priests, necessitate reliance in some measure upon the community's "pool" of secularly-employed priests.

The emphasis on ceremonial performance that is implied is not inadvertent. The fact is that whatever the breadth or scope of their education, the number of priests is insufficient to allow freedom from scheduled liturgical duties for the performance of other tasks appropriate to clerical vocation. Apparently, in earlier times, the situation was otherwise. A famous 9th century treatise in Pahlavi, *Dadistan-i Denik*, cites authoritative traditional opinions as sources for a summary of the characteristics of an ideal priest. However important

[5]The informant was Dr. Firoze Meherji Kotwal, when he was Principal of M.F. Cama Athornan Institute (Madressa), Andheri, Bombay, in personal interview, October 20, 1971. Dr. Kotwal has been—since May 1977—high priest (and Dastur) of Wadiaji Atash-Beheram Fire-Temple, Bombay.

[6]The prospect is *so* bleak, in fact, that in Iran the principle of heredity has already been breached, and the possibility of opening the priestly calling to all Zoroastrians has reached the open discussion stage in India. See Chapter 6.

the ability to perform all rituals faultlessly, the summary—as translated by a present-day Parsi scholar—shows that personal qualities of relevance for other functions were not left out of account. Thus an ideal priest was to be

> . . . of pure disposition, of innate wisdom, extraordinarily versed in religious scriptures, mediator of God, of spiritual vision, of pure thoughts, of truthful utterances, of righteous actions, pure of body, of sweet tongue . . . [7]

Today, such traits are not expected, nor have they been for most of this century, so that Modi could conclude, "A good deal of the original lofty ideal seems to have been lost now."[8] This is understandable if a priest's function is almost exclusively that of ritualist. The few priests who constitute exceptions are the high-priests of the most patronized and well-staffed temples. They are primarily administrators and, freed from having to share equally with their subordinates in the round of rites associated with the gahs, they sometimes preach or lecture, hold classes for the religious education of the laity, write tracts or manuals to encourage religious literacy, and provide pastoral counseling to those who trust in their wisdom to aid in the resolution of personal problems. Some of the high-priests possess, further, such prestige as a result of personal qualities and scholarly achievements that their employing boards of fire-temple trustees confer upon them the honorific title of *Dastur*.[9]

[7]Maneck F. Kanga, "The Concept of an Ideal Priest," *Iran Society Silver Jubilee Souvenir Volume* 1944-1969 (Calcutta : Iran Society, 1970), n. 1, p. 183. The author, an Avestan and Pahlavi scholar of Bombay, was a Joint Honorary Secretary of the K.R. Cama Oriental Institute from 1958 to 1973.

[8]J.J. Modi, "The Parsi Priesthood," *Journal of the K.R. Cama Oriental Institute*, Vol. XXXI, 1937, p. 117 (hereafter cited as *JCOI*). The article is a republication of an earlier work shown by internal evidence to have been written in 1915.

[9]It has become a tradition for the few temples accustomed to bestowing the title of Dastur to appoint no one as high-priest who is not worthy of the added title. The office and title are then hereditary if their holder has a son deemed worthy of them. In Bombay, Dasturs have only that influence in the community beyond their own temple which their reputation gives them. In Gujarat and Iran, the office may invest a Dastur of the principal temple with authority over all priests of the agiaries of the whole community. Obviously, patterns vary. The Dastur of Patel Agiary in Poona represents a third pattern. He has no jurisdiction beyond his own temple in Poona, yet he has authority over priests serving agiaries in several other Indian cities.

The great majority of the priests, however, are neither trained nor innately qualified to enlarge their role by assuming instructional and pastoral responsibilities, and the laity appears no more ready to trust in their capacity to diversify their role than they are to attempt it.

There are many features of the profession that are interrelated, making the priesthood the phenomenon that it is today. One feature of importance is the training of the candidates. Traditionally, a priest chose those of his sons whom he thought suited for the profession and prepared them himself to meet the tests that would be administered by other priests of the community preliminary to ordination ceremonies. It was equally customary to entrust the youthful prospective priests to a community's authoritative high-priest or Dastur for part or substantially all of their preparation.

A more institutionalized and systematic effort to stimulate study of Avestan and Pahlavi languages and liturgies by priestly sons (and laymen as well) brought *madressas* (institutes) into existence in Bombay during the last half of the 19th century. Such schools were started also in Gujarat at Navsari and Udvada.

Two institutions of later origin provide the education for most of the present Parsi as well as the infrequent Iranian or English Parsi candidates for the priestly profession. The Athornan Boarding Madressa of Bombay (f. 1917) provides a standard education for priestly sons and the religious subjects essential to ordination. The other, the M. F. Cama Athornan Institute, had the distinction for many years of providing free education to all the sons of the priestly class who were sent to it, without regard for their eventual choices of occupation. Founded in Andheri, a suburb of Bombay, in 1923, it accepted its students after their *Navjote* initiation and gave them both their priestly training and a secular education through the 9th standard. By that time, the priestly training had been sufficient to qualify most of them for higher ordination, Martab. Regardless of whether a student intended the priestly or a secular vocation, he could stay on at the Institute for language study while receiving instruction in the secular subjects of the 10th and 11th standards at a nearby secondary school. He then left the Institute and, like those who completed only the 9th standard, entered upon a vocation or, if he wished and was qualified, proceeded to a college or university.

The Institute found its dual objectivies were mutually contradictory. That part of the instruction which upgraded the general education

of priests was the kind of instruction that encouraged disenchantment with the profession's routinized functions. It became a common
complaint among the Parsis that the less intelligent students who
could memorize by rote became their priests while the ablest students
eschewed the priesthood to choose secular occupations. The value
of the scheme was that it made secular education available to
priestly sons, but it did little to improve upon traditional training
for the priesthood *per se*, and so the profession was not made more
attractive for the Institute's best students. Modi had observed, several
years before the Institute was founded, that "a priest would like to
see his intelligent and educated sons taking up professions other
than of the priesthood."[10] Since the Institute did not succeed in
altering that attitude, it could still be said, with Boyce, a half century
later, that ". . . the ablest boys go into secular life unless, exception-
ally, one of them has a strong sense of religious vocation."[11]

The need to avert such results led finally in 1977 to revision of the
Institute's admissions policy and curriculum. Inasmuch, however, as
no plan could succeed as long as the compensation of priests was
inadequate, the new plan was drawn to address that problem too—
as we must address it before outlining the plan itself.

The low level of income for priests has been a sore point for years.
Income has traditionally consisted of a share of the offerings made
for fire-temple ceremonies together with the gratuities given by
families who employ a priest to perform the outer ceremonies for
initiations, weddings, and funerals. Modi estimated that emoluments
for mature and highly competent priests might average twice those
of novices, but said that only a high priest or a Dastur would be
likely to enjoy a relatively fixed and generally adequate income.[12]

That no significant improvement had been made despite the concern felt over many years is shown by the decision of the Trustees of

[10]J.J. Modi, "The Parsi Priesthood," *JCOI*, XXXI, p. 126. Two Dasturs,
Modi claimed, were the only priests in Bombay with University degrees (in
1915).

[11]Boyce, "Zoroastrianism," *HR II*, p. 234. Boyce's observation is corroborated by no less an authority than Dr. Jal F. Bulsara, Secretary of the Bombay
Parsi Panchayat, 1930-1941. According to him, "It is not merely fathers of
priestly lineage in secular occupations, but even priest-fathers who do not have
their sons trained for the priesthood if they are good for anything else." Personal interview, Bombay, October 21, 1971.

[12]J. J. Modi, "The Parsi Priesthood," *JCOI*, XXXI, pp. 125-126.

the Parsi Panchayat of Bombay, in 1970, to guarantee a novice priest Rs. 250 per month (not including gratuities), an increase of Rs. 25 per year, free board at a fire-temple, and a subsidy for housing.[13] Meanwhile, the priests' economic situation in Bombay had not been a unique one somehow connected with the size and urban setting of the faith's largest community. In Poona, too—the city having the second largest concentration of Zoroastrians—concerned behdins in 1966 organized the Poona Athornan Aid Trust (PAAT), the principal purpose of which was to raise a Mobed Fund for the material and educational benefit of priests and their families.

The need to rely upon special trusts has made obvious the failure of Parsi communities and especially such bodies as fire-temple boards to adjust conditions of priests' employment to conform to the best of secular practices. "They [the priests] don't have pension," a prominent Parsi and one-time Trustee of the Bombay Panchayat recently noted. "They don't have bonus. They don't have anything compared to what an industrial worker has. The result, therefore, is that they are discouraged from becoming priests."[14]

The issue, however, is not one simply of injustice. Laymen admit readily that the priests remain poor, but they also ask if the priests are worth more than they are paid. They note that the education of priests, completed as it normally is in adolescence, provides no exposure to the social sciences, humanities, and graduate professional courses that are requisite to theological sophistication, historical perspective, or skill in preaching, teaching, and pastoral service. The

[13]Information supplied by Kotwal in personal interview, October 16, 1971. The novice would thus be guaranteed about $35 per month at best before perquisites. According to Dastur N. Minochehr-Homji, however, not all of Bombay's active priests were made beneficiaries of this plan for subsidies. (The same is true of the Institute's subsidies of one hundred rupees monthly for Bombay mobeds with both ordinations. There were only ten such beneficiaries in 1975.) The Dastur avers, further, that the Petit Fasli Atash Kadeh (the single fire-temple in Bombay representing the Fasli sect), which he serves as high-priest, is also "probably the single one in India with a Trust Fund the income of which provides salaries . . ." and not only monies for temple maintenance. Interview of November 8, 1971.

[14]"Future Shock," *Parsiana*, November 1973, staff article based on interview with Shiavax R. Vakil, p. 16. See also Sanober Marker's "The Plight of the Priests," *Parsiana*, November 1975, p. 14, where a practicing priest quotes "the paltry sum of two to three hundred rupees a month" as still typical compensation.

laity's understanding, accordingly, is that priests are narrowly trained mechanical functionaries whose work guarantees some strictly spiritual benefits but is otherwise so routine, monotonous, and unrelated to the laity's secular life that it may be compensated at a rate appropriate to the alleged mediocrity of the incumbents.

"We are not surprised," wrote Moulton in 1917, "that the profession has ceased to be an object of ambition."[15] His inquiries led him to estimate that Bombay had about 750 priests, of whom perhaps as few as 50 maintained their qualifications for performing the inner liturgical ceremonies. The situation of late differs mainly in having merely deteriorated further, until, for all of India, there are only about 400 full time priests.[16] Boyce has found that in Iran, too, the vocational advantages afforded by secular education when compared with sinking priestly incomes have led sons to abandon the calling "wholesale." "There are no new entrants to the priesthood," she states categorically, "and little inducement for future ones." Thus, the likelihood is "that the priesthood in Iran will die out with the present generation."[17] She has been but little more sanguine about the prospects in India, where, for the same reasons she found in Iran, the avoidance of the profession by those with hereditary right to it bespeaks a "future that cannot be said to be hopeful for Zoroastrainism. . ."[18]

In other parts of the world, there are priests serving communities of Zoroastrians, not a few of them with Martab as well as Navar credentials, but none serving full time except in Hong Kong, Pakistan, Sri Lanka and East Africa.[19]

This is the larger background against which to view the Athornan Institute's "New Mobedi Oriented Course." The plan provides a seven-year program which only the student already intending to be-

---

[15]Moulton, *The Treasure of the Magi, op. cit.,* p. 140.

[16]Ervad Peshotan F. Peer (retired), of Bombay, in World Congress Paper on "The Zoroastrian Priesthood," *Parsiana,* August-November, 1978, p. 36.

[17]Boyce, "Zoroastrianism," *HR II,* p. 234.

[18]*Ibid.,* p. 235.

[19]Information given in letters from Framroze A. Bode, of Bombay and Hollywood, California, May 14, 1973 (*supra,* n. 52, p. 46); Cyrus P. Mehta, United Kingdom, May 5, 1973; Jamshed K. Pavri, Vancouver, B.C., Canada, June 20, 1973; and T.R. Sethna, Karachi, Pakistan, December 21, 1977. Dastur Bode is now primarily a lecturer and writer. Mehta and Pavri at the time of writing were officers of the Zoroastrian Association of Europe and the Zoroastrian Society of British Columbia, respectively.

come a full time priest should embark upon—and that, as in the past, when he is of an age for Navjote (usually from seven to nine or ten years of age). Gujarati, English, mathematics, and recital by memory of Avestan texts are constants in the curriculum. The Zoroastrian religion and Iranian history are to be studied for six of the seven years. A total of about one-fourth of the program is to be devoted to studies in world history, geography, hygiene; Persian, Avestan, and Pahlavi as languages; and the conduct of rituals and ceremonies. The features of the pattern which analysis points to as dominant are the heavy concentration on languages, a fairly exclusive emphasis on the Zoroastrian religion and its cultural settings, and completion of the program while the average student is still in his adolescence.

So far as inherent appeal is concerned, this curriculum probably has neither more nor less than that of any other school. Two strategies have been defined, however, to add appeal by indirection. The first is that of placing planned stress on the nobility of serving God and the laity—a responsibility of which the teaching staff and a once-a-month guest lecturer are to be forever mindful. The second means is one of offering tangible reward. The trustees will establish a savings account for each student upon entry and make a deposit of Rs. 100 per month for the seven years of study and the first 15 years of service. The accumulated sum (expected to be in excess of Rs. 50,000 or about $6,300) may then be withdrawn or reinvested and the interest used to supplement earned income. At the same time, the benefitting priest is allowed the option of continuing in, or resigning from, the profession. If, on the other hand, the course of study is not completed, or the profession is given up before the completion of 15 years of service for any reason other than disability, the whole account reverts automatically to the trust fund.

The intentions are clear: to concentrate the school's resources, financial and tutorial, on none except would-be priests; the recruitment of more candidates for the profession; and success in persuading most of the graduates of the program to remain in the profession for a significant portion of their lives. Several years must pass before the effects of the plan will be as clearly discerned as are the intentions of its architects. Meanwhile, it is important to realize that even at best, the plan will not multiply overnight the number of priests in service. There are also certain problems that are bound

to arise but which seem not to have been anticipated in advance.[20]
The bleak forecasts about the future of the priesthood are not yet,
therefore, rendered wholly obsolete. The profession is still in need of
all the remedial aid that can be given it if it is to be put on the road
to recovery and its health eventually restored.

The Role of the Laity

The relationship of the behdin to the fire-temple constitutes in a
sense the basic premise by reference to which Zoroastrianism derives
its understanding of the place of its laity. That relationship, already
briefly noted, is one of association, not membership Custom-
honoring behdins visit their neighborhood or preferred fire-temple
as frequently as possible—ideally at least once daily—to say their
own prayers and to worship by observing the priests conduct the
rite appropriate to the gah of the day. All Zoroastrian ceremonies
are dedicated to the good of persons, living or dead. When the beneficiary is a specific person, the ceremony will have been commissioned—that is, requested and paid for by a contribution to the
temple. If no one has asked for such a dedication, the scriptures and
prayers of the gah period are dedicated by the priests to the benefit
of persons of their choice or to all Zoroastrians generally.

Given the increasing secularism of their daily life in the modern
age, Zoroastrians who really frequent the fire-temples are diminish-

---

[20]See "Circular No. 1," Minutes of the August Meeting of the Managing
Committee of the M.F. Cama Athornan Institute and the M.M. Cama Education Fund Committee, for the Meeting of 3 November 1977, Bombay. Saving
the Institute's resources for concentration on priestly studies also means no
support for the student who would like to complete secondary school. If a student wishes to carry his education that far anyway, without aid, he will find to
his dismay that the Institute's curriculum is not publicly certified; he must make
up deficiencies in general subjects at another school and attend classes with
younger children in order to do so. The boy who is both gifted and committed
to the vocation is bound to take a dim view of this barrier to his becoming a
better educated person (and priest). If he is gifted but has discovered a talent
and an overwhelming desire to devote his life to other service, he may suspect
the barrier of having been deliberately devised to trap him in the priesthood by
making it easier to resign himself to it than to escape it. In that case, the defer-
red value of the savings account could appear to him as just more bait in the
trap. The planning committee apparently did not anticipate that the scheme
may invite this kind of reaction from the school's best students, some of whom,
if they succumb, will be unhappy despoilers of priestly morale, while others,
if they rebel and leave, may become the vocation's most astringent critics.

ing in number. The twice-yearly festivals falling in the spring and autumn, when congregational attendance is expected, may provide for many the only occasions they choose to utilize for observing temple-centered ceremonies. There remain the outer ceremonies— the rites associated with initiation, marriage, death, and seasons—as occasions for public religious observance, but these occur principally in homes, or in pavilions within compounds established by philanthropic donors for such purposes, and they serve today to remind Zoroastrians more of their ethnic than their religious identity and values.

As a result of the pattern of association with rather than membership in the fire-temples, behdins have no voice in the determination of the policies and practices of their primary institution. In Bombay, very few of the fire-temples have priests offering weekly classes in the Gathas for adults; fewer still, classes for the religious education of children.[21] For the wider community, there are opportunities for religious inquiry provided by several voluntary committees or organizations formed by concerned Zoroastrians, but their appeal remains minimal and their geographical coverage thin and uneven. In any case, there is a prevailing assumption, characteristically traditionalist, that the corpus of true belief and practice has been given once and for all, and fidelity to it—not the re-forming of it—is the primary mark of a good Zoroastrian. The behdin, in short—especially in India –has no institutionally legitimized power to influence the shape of theology, liturgical practice, definitions of morality, or even the financial management of religious institutions. Unless he is one of the few trustees in the self-perpetuating board of a fire-temple, or a member of a reform-minded voluntary association, his only alternatives to conformity in practice and uncritical learning are laxity and economic attrition as ways of challenging by inaction what he cannot influence by voice or vote.

The earliest and still-surviving voluntary organization with some lay support among Parsis of Bombay is the Rahnumae Mazdayasnan Sabha (Religious Reform Association) founded in 1852. Its aims Karaka has described as "the regeneration of the social condition of the Parsis and the restoration of the Zoroastrian religion to its pristine purity."[22] Like many such developments in the

---

[21]Minochehr-Homji, personal interview, November 3, 1971.
[22]Karaka, *History of the Parsis, op. cit.,* II, 230.

history of various religions, the notion that the original founder's time was the "Golden Age" of truth has been linked with the conviction that if the fossilization or corruption of truth is to be avoided and its relevance and application assured, it must be translated into contemporary language and action. Thus one of the Sabha's early projects involved translating Scriptures into the Gujarati that most Parsis knew, with the intention that the translations would be used in the liturgies for worship as well as for study. The weight of tradition, however, immobilized liturgical reform, and the few Parsi scholars who have elected to study the history and ancient texts of their religion have been too divided by differing objectives to be of practical effect.[23] Still striving for relevance, the Sabha sponsors a program of lectures, inquiry sessions, and elocution contests designed to "bridge the cultural, social and generation gap" that divides the Parsi community.[24]

A second organization, likewise serving the Parsis of Bombay, is the Jashan Committee, founded in 1907. The name derives from but one part of its program which has been that of sponsoring public ritual celebrations—i.e., Jashans—commemorating events significant in Zoroastrian history, birthdates or deaths of famous Zoroastrians, seasons, and holidays of the liturgical year, and all of the faithfuls' ancestors in general. Its concern for education was expressed by taking the initiative to provide instruction in Zoroastrianism in Parsi schools. But whatever its activities, the avowed purpose was the defense of orthodoxy by countering publicly any reformist ideas not found conforming with scripture, tradition, or

---

[23]The divergent issues have been (1) to secure evidence from the past that can be used to defend retention of unchanging traditions, (2) to secure evidence that changes have been wrought—some viable, some not—and to learn from them how best to effect renewal in the present, and (3) to know the past and to understand it for its own scholarly worth—an aim that has moved those who hold it to take their stance above the battle of orthodoxy *versus* reform lest their objectivity and hence their whole inquiry be vitiated by partisan struggle and its attendant rancor. No special powers of discernment are needed to see that the advantage of such differences lies with the "side" that favors doing nothing at all—which is, of course, the traditionalists' position

[24]Thus did Jehangir R. Patel express the purpose of the Sabha in his "Editor's Column," *Parsiana*, December-January 1975, p. 3. His judgment at that time was that the association might become "once again . . . a force in the community." (p. 4.) He later decided, he said in personal interview on December 2, 1977, that he had been overly optimistic.

custom.

The founders intended to make the Committee a membership organization, but they restricted control to a self-perpetuating committee of trustees who, after seventy years, were only three in number, eleven having died. With only about fifteen dues-paying members in the late 1970s, the Jashan Committee, one may conclude, has not proved to be the institution which the orthodox of Bombay would choose to represent them.

By and large, the other organizations in which the laity (including secularly employed persons of priestly lineage) may hold membership are concerned with cultivating social solidarity and improving the worldly lot of the Zoroastrian community. Zeal for religion may be urged as a means to these ends, but the organizations provide no arena for the exercise of lay initiative with respect to religion itself. There are exceptions, of course. Three atypical sects have formed during the last two centuries to defend their different calendars and the times each calendar sets for their ritual obligations. The *Shahanshahis* use a calendar one month behind that of the Zoroastrian traditionalists of Iran. Those favoring the old calendar as normative are *Kadmis*. Then, seeing the confusion caused by having different religious and secular calendars, the third sect, of *Faslis*, was formed to urge replacement of the older calendars by the present national calendar of Iran. These differences, however, have nothing to do with the substance of the religion, nor are the sects organizations in the ordinary sense. They may more properly be called schools of thought coincidentally institutionalized by reason of each fire-temple's having of necessity to choose one of them for its ritual calendar. The choice will in most instances have been made by the founding philanthropist(s), so that the lay clientele of a given temple are with few exceptions associated with the sect only by the accident of patronizing that temple for other unrelated reasons.

Ilm-e-Khshnoom—already described—represents another distinctive phenomenon. As a sect or movement, it is like the Sabha in having explicit concern for analyzing substantive religious issues and winning acceptance for its interpretations. For a time between 1974 and 1976 it was in decline and could not sustain publication of its magazine, *Parsi Avaz*. The sect hopes now, however, that the new bi-monthly journal, *Dini Avaz* (Religious Voice, privately launched in December 1975), and revived classes for teaching its doctrines will keep the movement alive and the community from losing one of its few institutional channels for the exercise of lay initiative and responsibility in matters specifically religious.

The generalization stands, then, that the laity at least until recently played a significant role only in institutions concerned with their general social welfare. To this end, they have organized a Zoroastrian Association (Anjuman) in virtually every town, city, or province in which Zoroastrians have settled whether in India or in the widely scattered and distant countries of other parts of the world.[25] Major objectives are those of raising the consciousness of being Zoroastrian, extending and strengthening acquaintance with others of the faith, educating the young and reminding the old about the traditions that give the faith its distinctiveness, and devising ways of meeting the exigencies arising in new or small communities from an absence of traditional institutions and their services. It is when the exigencies require improvisation that such Associations sponsor meetings for discussion and, after that, policy formulation and action on questions which, for the orthodox at least, seem to be primarily religious and therefore not properly subject to debate and pragmatic resolution by a community organization largely behdin in its constituency. Such questions are reserved for treatment in a later chapter, but it may be useful in the present context to cite as example the issue of whether or not non-Zoroastrians mourning a deceased Zoroastrian may remain or be required to withdraw when it is time for the priests to begin intoning the sacred texts of the funeral liturgies. The orthodox hold that the issue is one of faith and not mere social policy. Juddins, they say, contaminate the ritual fire and vitiate the power of prayer because of their "unbelief" and their non-observance of the prerequisite purification rites. But Zoroastrians in England and North America and most Iranis differ. They find such strictness impracticable and admit all mourners, permitting them to join the faithful in filing past the bier at the close of services and "even. . .to put sandalwood and incense on the fire burning next to [the] coffin."[26] The

[25]There are 58 Indian associations, most of them affiliated with the Federaration of the Parsi Zoroastrian Anjumans of India; an estimated 16 Iranian anjumans, and at least 13 in other countries (Pakistan, Bahrain, Kenya, Hong Kong, Singapore, Australia, England, Canada and United States).

[26]Mehta, letter of May 5, 1973, *op. cit.* Other correspondents writing of the practices of their coreligionists in Western communities report the same re-

examples of such contrary practices are numerous, and that they bear on doctrine seems undeniable. Their import in relation to the role of the laity appears equally clear. In the old established communities, lay sentiment about religious questions can spark controversy but what is done remains the province of the mobeds. In the new communities abroad, however, the lay majorities in the Associations are making decisions in response to their different circumstances and are thereby exercising previously unheard-of influence—without any reported instance of deterrence by their fellow members, the part-time priests—in shaping their faith for the future.

Only the seer may forecast whether or not such initiative will in any way affect the role of the laity in the old communities. Were Associations the important instruments for decision making by Zoroastrians in Gujarat, Bombay or Poona, they might take their cues from this form of organization and the significant role it allows the laity. But in these areas of greatest Zoroastrian population density, Panchayats have provided the machinery for looking after extra-temple interests of each community—not, however, without consequences for the faith too singular to be left out of account.[27]

The Bombay Panchayat provides the prime example of organization intended, on the one hand, to make issues related to personal and social welfare the jurisdiction of laymen, and to deal with issues either admittedly or not always admitted to be religious,—but in a manner which seems to provide a given Parsi community as a whole with less voice in its affairs than that afforded by Associations.

The Panchayat of Bombay in its earliest form consisted of "a self-constituted body of the elders and influential members of the

---

laxation of the traditional rules of exclusion, and the author of this work observed the same in Iran. No such revision of custom seems in prospect in Bombay or the towns of Gujarat.

[27] An exception to this conclusion may be provided by the situation in the so-called Mofussil (rural or isolated, and tending to remain traditional) settlements of Gujarat. While the Bombay Panchayat gradually extended its oversight of Parsis' social welfare to include the Mofussil area, it accepted the fact that its sphere of influence when dealing with more specifically religious issues was confined to Bombay. As Karaka noted in 1884, so during this century, "In religious matters ... the priests of Navsari [the "central shrine" of Mofussil towns] have held their own as the supreme authority up to this very day." *Op. cit.*, I, 217.

community. . . [serving as a] court of justice"[28] for the Parsi community. That it could authoritatively excommunicate and deny all priestly and religious services to anyone disobeying its decrees indicates its involvement in matters religious as well as social. Self-perpetuating thereafter until the late 18th century, it came to be regarded as representative of the interests of a privileged class, and the Governor for the British Government directed that a more representative organizational structure be devised. The result, in 1787, was a new Panchayat consisting of six priests and six laymen chosen by the "old" Panchayat from twenty-four persons suggested be various community leaders. No restriction of powers, however, was imposed. The purpose was still that of "adjudicating on all social and religious matters concerning the Parsis. . ."[29]

As might be expected, the Panchayat's history reflects the evolving circumstances of Bombay's Parsi community as a whole. Structurally, it has been modified, usually in order to make it somewhat more democratic and representative, to permit a limited number of women to become trustees, and to limit trustees' terms to ten years (unless re-elected).

Reorganization of the Panchayat, however, has not really resolved long-standing issues relating to the role of the laity in religious affairs. There was a period when, in an effort to clarify and define roles, the Panchayat was declared to be nothing more than a trustee of funds and properties useful to the Parsis' social well-being. Said Karaka, "For the last fifty years the. . . Panchayet is. . . powerless for either good or evil, and performs no other functions than those of trustee to certain charitable funds of the community."[30] Reading between the lines of various accounts, we perceive curious ambivalences. Originating as a body less designed to give the laity some religious authority than to reduce and finally make subordinate the priests' power in secular affairs, the Panchayat evolved as a self-perpetuating institution not only deciding questions implicitly religious but doing so essentially "on its own"—*i.e.* without being effectively bound by any structural machinery to heed the voice or

---

[28]Karaka, *op. cit.*, I, 217-218. Eckehard Kulke gives 1673 as the year of founding for the first Panchayat. *The Parsees*, A Bibliography on an Indian Minority, with introduction (Freiburg, 1968), pp. xvii-xviii.

[29]Karaka, *op. cit.*, I, 223.

[30]*Ibid.*, pp. 240-241.

the will of the laity allegedly represented. If Karaka was right in his assessment of the mid-19th century situation as one of powerlessness, it was because such a Panchayat had lost the trust of the laity to whom it did not listen. Also, and simultaneously, the English colonial administration was applying an increasingly standardized code of law to formerly semi-autonomous ethnic and religious communities and thus diminishing the capacity of their agencies to translate distinctive doctrinal tenets into social practice.

Nevertheless, the limitation on powers was in some respects more apparent than real, for the Panchayat was not without the will or the resources for employing litigation to seek decisions from the English courts that it could not impose by itself. The "Parsi Punchayet Case" of 1906 (decided in 1908) is the most famous of cases in point. The refined and respected French wife of R.D. Tata had converted to Zoroastrianism and been duly initiated by a high-priest. Knowing however that the prevailing orthodoxy of the time would favor denial to Mrs. Tata of religious as well as social rights and privileges accorded to hereditary Parsis, Tata and five friends sued to enjoin the Panchayat Trustees from refusing to the convert any of the benefits from the trusts under Panchayat management that were available to Parsi Zoroastrians. The presiding judge found no legal excuse for voiding the intention of donors who had clearly named *Parsis* as exclusive beneficiaries. He used the occasion, however, to excoriate the defendants in trenchant terms for subordinating religion to caste prejudice and thus, by indirection at least, shaping the religion in accord with arguments that were "mere frippery and shallow sophistry."[31]

If Karaka would have been surprised to see the Panchayat retaining in religious matters an influence which he thought it no longer exercised, the Joint Secretary of the Panchayat, S.F. Desai, would have been well advised in 1963 not to echo Karaka's assessment of its role without admitting of the possibility that occasions like that of the case of 1906 might recur.[32] A resolution passed by

[31]"The Parsi Punchayet Case, In the High Court of Judicature at Bombay, Suit No. 689 of 1906." Judgment of the Hon'ble Mr. Justice Beaman. 27 November, 1908. Printed at the Bombay Gazette Electric Printing Works, 1908, p. 32.

[32]Sapur Faredun Desai, *The Parsi Panchayet and its Working,* Revised and enlarged (Bombay: 1963). "Today," wrote Desai, "its motto is to serve, its

the trustees in 1974, was one such occasion. The English daughter-in-law of a noted Iranian Zoroastrian had attended his funeral cere-monies in a *bungli* (bungalow) at Doongerwadi until asked by the presiding priests to withdraw.[33] Responding to othodox sentiment, the Panchayat's trustees "convened a special urgent board meeting and passed the resolution which required family members to sign a statement . . . that non-Parsis would not be permitted to enter the bunglis while the prayers were in session." Included also was the request that the mobeds perform no part of a funeral ceremony in the presence of a non-Zoroastrian.[34] While mounting counter-criticism soon effected rescission, the resolution nonetheless illustrates the Panchayat's singular position as the Bombay Parsis' one essentially-lay institution capable of action and not mere agitation with respect to questions religious as well as social. Yet, say its critics, its structure has not been sufficiently modified to give rank and file Parsis powers of influence comparable to those exercised by an economically advantaged oligarchy. In consequence, the critics continue, Zoroastrianism's largest lay community has little voice in defining the contemporary shape and expression of the faith. For, while it is true that the oligarchy may be chiefly behdin in com-position, its decisive support has so far been given to orthodoxy, and how the community might express itself were it encouraged to do so remains obscure. In other words, if the few behdins with influence sound consistently like orthodox priests, there is little war-rant yet for regarding the role of laity in general as a significant component of the institutional power structure.

This is like neither of the situations found in the Iranian and emigrant communities. The decline of the priestly profession in Iran has left some communities without priests, so that the laity are in complete control of their religious and communal affairs. Lay control is exercised also in the communities served by priests recruited from India, since it would seem presumptuous of these priests to impose Parsi norms on Zoroastrians and their institutions in the land of the religion's birth.

The newer Western communities are not quite like those of either

---

main function to maintain and manage funds and properties . . . to be more a charitable or relief-giving institution than [!] a socio-religious body." p. 8.

[33]See *infra*, n. 12, and n. 34, Chap. IV.

[34]"The Doongerwadi Ban," *Parsiana*, May 1974, pp. 12-13.

India or Iran. The allocation of authority is hardly an issue with them. Because there are no full time priests and no consecrated fire-temples, rules and customs applicable elsewhere become little more than guidelines if relevant at all, and dead letters if apparently irrelevant. Part time priests who are held in high respect may be encouraged to participate in governance, but if it is thought they will have nothing to contribute, the laity ask from them only the performance of the outer ceremonies.

What these differing patterns of defining powers and roles for the Anjumans (and their lay members) augur as to the future of Zoroastrianism is difficult to predict. What may be safe to say is that such differences tend to make only forums of discussion out of the periodic World Congresses that Zoroastrians have taken to holding, thereby postponing the day when such congresses can be legislative bodies capable of unifying and giving forceful direction to the worldwide fellowship.

Religious Education

The organization of ecclesiastical instrumentalities for religious education is so commonplace an activity for many religions that it occasions some surprise to discover that Zoroastrianism has evolved no comprehensive plan or structure of official agencies for this purpose. Normally, a religious education program might be expected to have as its concerns the communication of the history of the faith, explanations of its contemporary meaning and relevance, and provision for meaningful discussion and debate capable of issuing in further theological, organizational, and ethical development. Zoroastrians have these concerns, especially the first one; what they lack are effective official agencies to express them.

The principal form of the Zoroastrian educational organization is the voluntary association of individuals sharing a common purpose. Those whose interest in occult doctrine impels them to attend classes and to subscribe to the privately funded journal that expounds the views of Ilm-e-Khshnoom comprise in an informal way this otherwise unstructured sect. The Rahnumae Sabha has the somewhat more formal structure of a membership organization guided by two honorary secretaries, a few well known leaders including priests, and a managing committee. Its purposes make it an agency for religious education, but its voluntary membership principle and small following provide it with no authority or definitive jurisdiction.

It is merely some leaven of reform in the loaf of traditionalism. And as for the many local Panchayats, Anjumans, or Associations, we have seen that their concerns, historically, have been the social well-being of the community and preservation of a sense of Zoroastrian identity. They have favored religious education but have done little either to sponsor it or otherwise encourage it by systematically planning and underwriting a publication program.

One organization not hitherto mentioned but one that has had the potential for developing a sturdy structure and a clearcut program is the Athornan Mandal (Priest Association) of Bombay. Founded in 1915 and meeting quarterly, it could conceivably have become an effective agency of religious education. It chose, however, to pursue objectives mainly ameliorative: to resolve sectarian differences, dissolve hostility between priestly families of different Panthaks, and overcome personal animosities engendered by minor ideological differences. For a time, the desire to encourage more priestly sons to elect the priestly vocation prompted the Mandal to favor more advanced education for priests, in the thought that this would increase respect for the vocation and attraction to it. Unfortunately, "disenchantment with the idea" set in when it was noted that those of their youthful candidates or ordinees who went on to university were inclined to choose other vocations.[35]

Two reasons may be advanced in explanation of why the Mandal has not become an educational agency or even a self-educating forum of discussion and debate. The first is that only about half of Bombay's priests are members of the Mandal, and one-third of those, says Ervad Bajan, are men with secular vocations and only an avocational interest in performing ceremonies. The organization cannot claim, therefore, to speak authoritatively even for the religious professionals of the community. The second reason is that attendance at meetings is insufficient for the purpose of securing agreement by a recognizable majority for either the definition of policy or the support of a program. Nor can attendance improve as long as a sizable contingent of full time priests must always be absent from meetings in order to attend to the temple ceremonies of the gah of the day that coincides with the Mandal's meeting time.

[35]Interview with Ervad Jal A. Bajan, head priest of Karani Agiary, Bombay, and for thirty years Honorary Secretary of the Athornan Mandal, December 1, 1971.

In summary of the priestly role in education, the priests trained to foster an educational program in their own temples are too few to challenge effectively the prevailing religious illiteracy. Furthermore, because most of them do not view teaching as germane to their role anyway, they have made no collective effort through the Mandal to foster an educational program. "In Bombay," says Marker, "the Athornan Mandal was formed to aid the priests but it is moribund."[36]

One means of spreading religious literacy is that of the printed word, together with a professionally planned publication program. For Zoroastrianism, however, there is no such program—a situation due, again, to lack of ecclesiastical machinery or corporate structure. Therefore, the use of publications to be informative and instructive in a systematic way is largely the function of commercial enterprises. The best known vehicles are the newspapers published by Parsis depending upon Parsi readers to account for the bulk of their circulation. Obviously, a high concentration of Zoroastrians is necessary to make such ventures profitable, and Bombay is accordingly the community able to support the reformist weekly *Kaiser-e-Hind*, a bilingual Gujarati-English tabloid, and the orthodox daily *Jam-e-Jamshed*, in Gujarati.[37] Primarily general news media, they serve as instructional media as well to the extent that their editorials, feature stories or articles, and letter columns provide forums for debating issues of significance for Zoroastrian religion and life.

The second type of publication is the newspaper or journal sponsored by individuals (one or more) or organized associations. The objective is primarily educational rather than merely informative. The tone may be either partisan or impartial. The weekly newspaper, *Parsi Avaz*, now succeeded by the bimonthly Gujarati-English journal, *Dini Avaz*, is illustrative of the private publication with sponsors either willing to subsidize it for the sake of their sectarian cause or hopeful of meeting costs by securing advertising and subscribers. Similarly non-commercial but essentially impartial or scholarly, are the K.R. Cama Oriental Institute's periodical *Journal* and occasional monographs funded from the Institute's endowment, and

---

[36]Sanober Marker, "The Plight of the Priests," *op. cit.*, p. 17.

[37]A third newspaper, the reformist daily, *Bombay Samachar*, may be left out of account. Although Parsi owned and edited, it appeals mainly to non-Parsi Gujarati readers.

Dipanjali, the half-yearly journal supported from the budget of the Delhi Parsi Anjuman.

A maverick among these types is the English language journal, *Parsiana*. Founded in 1964 and edited by P.B. Warden, a physician, for discussion of any issue of interest to Parsis, it was given the needful transfusion of a new publisher and editor, Jehangir R. Patel, in August 1973. Whether or not its now thoroughly professional journalistic excellence will attract sufficient subscribers to assure solvency remains to be seen. In any event, it is quite the brightest of current Parsi periodicals and the one best calculated to provoke enlightened rather than merely sagely repetitious or frivolously iconoclastic discussion about old issues—or, for that matter, new ones.

The journalistic organs for Iranians are the Persian language monthlies, *Hukht* and *Mehname Zartoshtiyan*. The latter is somewhat like *Time* or *Newsweek* except that it concentrates on Zoroastrian news and views. It is *Hukht* which seeks to educate, by its articles devoted to history, contemporary religious and social issues, and comparative religion.

There is finally the category of books and booklets to characterize. Perhaps the most obvious trait of these is unevenness of quality. Since there is no Zoroastrian official press and both Iran and India in general have but few prestigious commercial publishing companies, there is no well-established tradition of having submitted manuscripts refereed, recommended, and finally professionally edited for publication. The rare, respected scholar-writer may be fortunate in finding a Western publisher of distinction. The same scholar, or one somewhat wanting in credentials but still enjoying respect from a community that is not rigorously critical, may be the beneficiary of sponsorship by some Parsi educational trust, the trustees or managers of which see merit in his work. But most Indian Parsis—and they are almost alone among the world's Zoroastrians who write about their religion for publication—are more motivated by zeal to instruct than by scholarly competence or literary skill. The result is the appearance from time to time of a new treatise initially subsidized by its own writer or by a fellow religionist of means. As elsewhere in the world, the temperament of persons who acquire wealth is often sympathetic to a partnership with conservatism generally. It is not surprising, therefore, to find that most of the publications privately subsidized or supported by philanthropy are apologies for whatever has been made a part of the religious tradition by longtime acceptance and practice. These are the works most often given free distribution or stocked by book stores with Parsis among their clientele. Conversely, the reformers who possess wealth or enjoy patronage are few, so that for diffusion of their views they must depend upon brief inexpensive tracts or acceptance of short articles and letters by editors of newspapers and magazines.

There are doubtless some omissions from this survey of what Zoroastrians write for Zoroastrians, but their inclusion is hardly necessary to show that the religion receives somewhat less support from the printed word than could be given by a professionally planned, coordinated, and well managed publications program. A rationally ordered program would make available to the community the works of scholars, journalists, creative writers, and religious educators whose concerns would be to increase religious knowledge, revitalize convictions, and deepen commitments. The emergence of such a program, however, will have to depend upon either the prior or simultaneous evolution of a comprehensive interrelated set of boards, committees, or commissions of representative character and institutionally unifying effectiveness.

The Panchayats or Anjumans, with their relatively narrow functions, are unlikely to evolve into the agencies that would overcome institutional atomism; but they, or a world Zoroastrian organization, were it ever organized, might serve catalytically to inspire construction by suggesting ways of taking first steps, however small. Some Parsis hoped that the Second World Zoroastrian Congress in 1964 might be such an agent. But its report, suggesting among other things a synchronized world-wide effort to ease the "plight of the priesthood" is presumed to be "lying [dead] in the files of the Parsi Panchayat, Bombay."[38] One "brainchild" of the Congress that *was* born—finally, in December 1971 – is the Federation of the Parsi Zoroastrian Anjumans of India. Hopes for its effectiveness, however, were somewhat dashed when requests that particularly pressing issues—such as the problems of the priesthood—be seriously addressed were declared too "delicate" or "controversial" for its

---

[38]From a letter written to the Executive Council of the Federation of Parsi Zoroastrian Anjumans by high priests H.K. Mirza and K.M. JamaspAsa, and quoted in "No Mobeds, No Parsis," a *Parsiana* staff article, issue of February 1976, p. 15.

Executive Council to discuss.[39] The Council's tack, it seems, is non-interference with problems that autonomous member Anjumans are urged to solve for themselves—an approach hardly cheering to those Parsis who were envisioning a "dynamic body to get on with the job of solving the problems facing the community."[40]

It was the Council of this Indian Federation that planned the Third World Zoroastrian Congress held in Bombay in January 1978. The meeting served, for the most part, to underline the fact that tradition will exercise authority in the absence of institutions with decision-making powers. In any case, the Congress had no such authority, for it was a gathering, not a body of delegated representatives with power to legislate. The majority of the members of the Council had voted to allow limited comment but not discussion of controversial issues. The only concrete results, therefore, were (1) the formation of an unofficial ad hoc "Standing Publications Committee" by several delegates whose concern was "to look into ways of developing materials for [the] religious education of children," and ([2]) an official resolution directing the planners of the Congress to draw up a constitution for a permanent "World Body."[41]

Implementation of the resolution would give Zoroastrians the first high-level, representative, coordinating institution of their history. Any possibility of early action, however, was quickly nullified. The Congress had hardly adjourned when the trustees of the Bombay Panchayat voted to secede from the Indian Federation. Their example was followed by several other member Anjumans, making it a foregone conclusion that the Council of the decimated Federation would have problems more parochial than global to monopolize its attention. One would have to be a saoshyant with a seer's gift of vision to foretell a time when the will to cooperate in planned action overcomes the inertia of traditionalism.

[39]"The Lady and the Letter," a *Parsiana* staff article, March 1975, pp. 11, 12, 44.

[40]*Ibid.*, p. 44, quoting editorial opinion of the Delhi-based Zoroastrian journal, *Dipanjali* (n.d.).

[41]Unpublished report of the Third World Zoroastrian Congress, Bombay, January 4-8, 1978, by Lovji D. Cama, President of the Zoroastrian Association of Greater New York.

CHAPTER 4

The Cultus

No aspect of Zoroastrianism is more difficult to describe and summarize than is its ritual structure or cultus. The number and variety of rituals and the manifold details of their performance and repetition account for most of the difficulty. There are rites for every day, every season, every phase of human life, and almost every human action. One can say that, in theory at least, all of life is ritual, and for the priests in particular it would be true in practice as well as theory. It is no wonder, then, that J. J. Modi needed 484 pages (exclusive of Index) for his monumental work, *The Religious Ceremonies and Customs of the Parsis* (1922), and that no one else before or after him has aspired to equal eminence as an authority on the history, meaning, and rubrics of the cultus.

The importance traditionally assigned to the cultus provides further occasion for difficulty in doing it justice. Zoroastrians can debate many issues of historical, theological, ecclesiastical, and ethical import without seeming to believe that all is lost if agreement is not reached. But the would-be reformer of the cultus finds himself opposing a phalanx of priests and laity arrayed against any suggestion that change be effected. Changes have occurred, of course, and others are in process. The transition made by most Zoroastrians from rural to urban living, and to modernity, has made many a feature of the traditional rites either anachronistic or impossible to preserve. Acceptance of change for such cause can be accepted, yet not without travail of soul. What cannot so readily be tolerated is the notion that innovations may be deliberately introduced. And what cannot be tolerated at all is the suggestion that the cultus might be less than absolutely efficacious in assuring access to God and in veritably upholding the world.

The cultus, then, is constituted of such a staggering bulk of ceremonial detail with imputed sacrosanctity that its summary is peculiarly hazardous. Perhaps the best that one can do is provide glimpses here and there of the types of ritual and the assumptions underlying their practice, and hope that a fuller account of a few rites will prove more informative than misleading as to the whole.

Viewed in historical perspective, the cultus echoes in part Zoroaster's expurgated versions of the old Indo-Iranian rituals but harks back even more to forms and practices revived or developed by the Magi after the prophet's time.

Almost certainly inherited by Zoroaster were the fire cult, the Haoma cult, and animal sacrifice (of cow or bull), all of which were too established to ignore but not beyond Zoroaster's capacity to reform. If we may give credence to Modi's understanding that "Agiary," a commonly used term for fire-temple, means "the place of Ag, Agni or fire,"[1] then we must surely also suppose Agni (or the more familiar Atar in Iran) held a place of prominence in the pre-Zoroastrian Indo-Iranian panoply of deities comparable to that of the same Agni in the Indo-Aryan and subsequent Hindu traditions. Zoroaster's reforming contribution would be that he brought fire into service as the earthly symbol *par excellence* of the wisdom and righteousness of Ahura Mazda, or, as Taraporewala would have it, reduced the status of Atar as a deity by making fire simply the principle *symbol* of the Zarathushtrian faith.[2]

Iranians before Zoroaster's time had also shared with the Aryans the discovery of the plant with the intoxicating juice, haoma (San-

---

[1] Modi. *RCCP*, p. 262.

[2] Taraporewala, *The Religion of Zarathushtra*, p. 40. Concerned to establish Zoroaster as a "strict monotheist," Taraporewala resisted admitting that the fire, Atar, might have been "personified" in the thinking of Zoroaster. His 1947 translation of the Gathas, included in the 1965 edition of the work just cited, seems to reflect this viewpoint. ". . . unto Thine INNER FLAME I pay / My homage . . . " (Yasna 43:9) is his version (p. 114) of what James Hope Moulton, following for the most part other respected authorities, renders "At the gift of adoration to thy Fire . . ." See his *Early Zoroastrianism* (London: Williams and Norgate, 1913), p. 366. Whether intentional or not, the Taraporewala translation makes the "flame" a symbol for an inner character trait, whereas the "fire" of other versions is clearly a real and external fire. A real fire may also be understood principally as a symbol for a moral or spiritual value or state, but it was vulnerable to personification—even deification— as well; and this, it seems, Taraporewala wanted no one to think Zoroaster ever did. Had he accepted the usual translation, he could still have argued just as plausibly that Zoroaster ignored Atar as a divinity and related fire solely to the worship of Ahura Mazda.

skrit : soma), deifying and worshipping it as the source of new life, of health and healing, and of immortality. An analogical connection between ecstasy by intoxication and that experienced as a spiritual state was perceived by most peoples of the ancient world and in Iran it may be supposed that Haoma was worshipped as a deity by devotees of the ahuras as well as by the propitiators of the daevas. The Gathas provide few clues to Zoroaster's attitude except that he vigorously denounced the worship of daevas and the overindulgence that issued in drunkenness and licentiousness. Presumably, therefore, he retained the use of the plant as a modest stimulant in the context of the sacramental ritual centered upon Ahura Mazda.[3]

A similar conclusion is generally thought warranted with respect to Zoroaster's views of animal sacrifice. Unless words are put in his mouth that are not in the Gathas, his objection was not to such sacrifice itself but to the prodigal waste of oxen in great numbers, to the wanton cruelty with which they were slaughtered, and to the magical notions crudely substituting physical strength and ebullience for higher spirituality as a religious objective.[4]

Once the Magi had established themselves as the spokesmen and priests of the Mazdayasnian religion, they confirmed the drift back to sacerdotal ritualism and polytheism that seems to have set in soon after Zoroaster's death. Already in the early post-Gathic Yasna—the most important liturgical text for Zoroastrianism—the pre-Avestan Haoma had regained the status of deity that had slipped toward mere personification, to be addressed there (and to this day) as a god, divine self-immolating victim, and prototypal priest. The one significant difference between his pre-Zoroastrian and later Avestan fortunes is that he lost his independence in rehabilitation; his cult was accommodated to Avestan Zoroastrianism by giving him Ahura Mazda for a father.

Sraosha had a somewhat similar if simpler metamorphosis. In the Gathas sraosha means hearing and obeying. Ahura Mazda listens to prayer and man, hearing His response, obeys. But as personification became more palpable in the later Avestan period, Sraosha acquired status as a messenger communicating God's word to man and the punisher of any who will not listen. Once given

[3]See Zaehner, *Dawn and Twilight*, pp. 84-90.
[4]*Ibid.*

god-like responsibilities, he was the only divinity besides Haoma to whom a special Yasht (hymn of praise) was dedicated. His stature has been further enhanced in post-Avestan times by promotion and increased responsibilities. Now "ruler of this earth as the Wise Lord is the ruler of the spiritual world above,"[5] he is also honored as aide, guide, and one of the three judges of the souls of the righteous dead.

The one cult which, while accounting for a share of the corpus of ritual as re-expanded after Zoroaster's reform, nevertheless very nearly vanished was the cult of animal sacrifice. Whether Zoroaster abhorred it in its entirety or adapted it after eliminating its vulgarities, historians agree that his later followers restored it, excesses and all. Apparently, however, the prophet's critique was not altogether forgotten, for the excesses disappeared from Zoroastrian ritual practice after the Muslim conquest of Iran and the slaughter of animals for sacrifice ceased completely among the Parsis by mid-19th century.[6]

The Yasna ceremony as embellished by its priestly practitioners has remained central in the ritual system. Other rites honoring old Iranian deities re-certified by catholic Zoroastrianism were added and correlated with the calendar, the passage of days, seasons, and years thus providing a steady succession of occasions requiring ritual observance and the Yashts of the *Avesta* providing the texts. Magian dominance of the religion also supplied the exaggerated and compulsive concern for purity which dictated the Videvdat and inspired the proliferation of purificatory rites. The correlation of these with life's transitional experiences such as religious initiation, marriage, and death, and also with many a normal daily activity, completes the process of sacralizing almost all of life for the pious or orthodox Zoroastrian.

The historical evolution of the cultus began, then, with Zoroaster's adaptation of old Iranian rites—by reinterpretation and pruning—to

---

[5] *Ibid.*, p. 96.

[6] See Boyce, "Haoma, Priest of the Sacrifice," *W. B. Henning Memorial Volume*, eds. Mary Boyce and Ilya Gershevitch (London: Asia Major Library: Lund Humphries, 1970) p. 67. Ritual consecration of "bread, water, milk and wine, plants and animal products" goes back at least to Avestan times, but "on solemn occasions an animal is sacrificed," says Boyce. The practice, she assures us, "still continues in th᾿ most orthodox villages of Iran." *Ibid.*

the end that they might cultivate and celebrate the religious experience and moral life of Mazdayasnians. However, with leadership passing to a hereditary priestly caste during the Achaemenid period, the era of ritual economy was over. Neglected rites were revived, and new ones were added as scriptural texts multiplied and supplied their justifications and liturgies. Yet Zoroaster's monotheistic spirit had left its mark, and all religious acts would henceforth be "first devoted to Ahura Mazda, whatever the dedication of the particular service."[7]

As for the cultus in general, it suffered with the decline of faith that occurred in all but the principal strongholds of Zoroastrianism during the early centuries of Muslim rule. Even in India, the situation was much the same. Communication was broken and not restored until the end of the fifteenth century when the Parsis began sending emissaries to Iran to ask questions about the proper conduct of rituals. Question and answer tracts known as *The Persian Rivayats* were the results of such missions, and by the eighteenth century the Parsis were reasonably well informed concerning departures from Persian traditions that time and circumstance had fostered. The Parsis were not about ready, however, to return in every instance to presumably older Persian ways. The majority of them had become urban residents and cosmopolitan in their outlook. Many minutiae the meanings of which were either forgotten or lacking more contemporary justification continued to be ignored by the Parsis. Similar tendencies toward simplification and rationalization have more recently appeared in Iran and in the new communities of the West, with encouragement provided by a shortage of priests and the will to survive.

Persisting Leitmotifs

Zoroastrian ritualism is given its special character by devotion to purity. The ideal is a blend; physical purity is not only highly valued along with purity of heart or soul, but the two kinds of purity are made so interdependent as to be—to the Zoroastrian— indistinguishable. According to Modi, "As religion powerfully impresses upon the mind of the masses the necessity of preserving laws of health and purification, their observation has taken the form

[7]Boyce, *BSOAS, XXXIII,* Part I, p. 36.

of religious ceremonies."[8]   Purity is thus both end and means—the quality or state of character most nearly synonymous with right- eousness, the proper temporal goal of human striving, and at the same time the condition most requisite to gaining the favor of God and acceptance into his Kingdom at the final judgment.

The principal symbolic artifacts of the ritual system are fire, water, haoma, urine, milk or ghee, and bread. Of these, the most prominent is fire, for it symbolizes as does its macrocosmic proto- type, the sun, the God whose light and wisdom bestow life and establish truth. Furthermore, once kindled and consecrated in a temple, a fire may be moved but never extinguished. The first four of the symbols named are normally regarded as potent purifying agents. Yet they can themselves be impure or be made so. Conse- quently, such symbolic artifacts must be consecrated after purifica- tion processes of varying complexity in order to offer assurance that their effect will be cleansing and revivifying, in turn, for the worshippers. As illustration, water for purification purposes in ritual should be drawn only from wells and contained in vessels that are not of porous material until used to cleanse a body or other objects. Temple fires, of which there are three grades, seem to differ less in degree of purity than of sanctity, yet the special potency of fire as a consumer or destroyer of impurities does not render it itself immune to contamination. Hence, the use of the *padan*, a two-layered cloth covering the nose and mouth, to prevent the priest's exhaled breath or his saliva from defiling the fire or other ritual artifacts. In India, where ideas about physical and religious purity are most mingled, the mere presence of a non-Zoroastrian in a place consecrated for liturgical use—even if the juddin be in the finest of health, freshly bathed, and sinless by the standards of another religion—is commonly regarded as contaminating to the ritual artifacts and the spiritual influence which the sacred place would otherwise exert upon the character of worshipping Zoro- astrians.

The centers or sites for the conduct of rites as practiced today possess sanctity in degrees varying according to the relative need

[8]Modi, *RCCP*, p. 90. Modi also cites J. Darmesteter's comment that Zoroas- trians go beyond treating cleanliness as next to godliness and make "cleanliness" ...a form itself of godliness." *Ibid.*, quoting from *Le Zend Avesta*, II, Intro- duction, (Paris, 1892-3), p. x.

for purity. The so-called "inner" liturgical services require a location in which ritually clean priests, practicing Zoroastrians, and cultic artifacts will not be defiled by persons or things that are not cultically pure. The fire-temple provides such a location, and in India, where juddins are excluded from temples, the chamber for housing the sacred fire is so positioned that juddins can not even *see* it from any position outside. Although properly speaking this chamber alone is called the *Dar-i-Mihr* (the porch of Mithra), the term is not infrequently used to denote the whole temple. The more common term for the temple is agiary, the place of fire.

Another site restricted out of consideration for purity is the *Bareshnumgah*, the place where the Bareshnum,[9] a personal purification ceremony, is held. Originally intended as a rite preliminary to priestly ordination and for anyone seriously defiled, the Bareshnum today is "taken" almost exclusively by priestly sons before ordination, by any priest with Martab ordination whose Bareshnum has been vitiated by failure to observe all the rules applicable to his vocation,[10] and by professional corpse bearers before they take up that occupation and, again, if they leave it. The rule requiring an isolated site is not now enforced, and it is commonplace to utilize for the Bareshnumgah an area of a fire-temple's grounds secluded enough to prevent approach or observation of the nude candidate and the two presiding priests.[11]

[9] *Infra*, pp. 94-96.

[10] Rather curiously, while Navar priests must go through two Bareshnum ceremonies preceding ordination, they do not hold Bareshnum qualification until after their third Bareshnum and ordination as Martab priests. Only Martab priests may perform the "inner" liturgical ceremonies, and then only if they "hold" the Bareshnum—*i.e.* have not vitiated it by "1. Eating of food cooked by non-Zoroastrians. 2. Non-observance of the Baj [the mini-ritual associated with bathing, meals, and calls of nature]. 3. Long travels and voyages. 4. Swearing or taking [civil] oaths. 5. Falling off of the [white priestly] turban from over the head." Modi, *RCCP*, p. 148. Qualification is restored by repeating the Bareshnum rite.

[11] Modesty prompts the exclusion of observers in general, but purity can not be left out of account as a major consideration. Since a Bareshnum is conducted by two priests, themselves "pure," in order to purify a third person— one who, moreover, may be a candidate for Martab and thereafter a purifier of others—it becomes a *sine qua non* to prevent the certain defilement that would result from the presence or proximity of known sources of pollution, namely ruleless non-Zoroastrians and rule-neglecting Zoroastrians.

Indian Parsis also protect the grounds of *dakhmas* and bunglis (bungalows, for funeral services), although the restrictions apply more to time than to place. Juddins may view the body of a deceased friend before the professional corpse tenders have begun their work of preparing it for last rites. They are thereafter excluded from the room until both the preparation and the succeeding funeral service are completed. They may stand outside and at a respectful distance, however, to betoken farewell when the Zoroastrian mourners escort the bier in procession to the dakhma.[12]

The concern for purity and the employment of some principal symbols are found wherever and for whatever purpose there is ritual, but ordinarily the condition of sites is inconsequential as compared with that of persons. The home and the "parish hall" with adjoining open court are common ritual sites, but neither of these is restricted territory, and only the Zoroastrian principals involved in a rite, and properties for personal use, are normally governed by rules enjoining purity. Thus the main purpose of such rules at the time of childbirth is to restore purity to the mother, and, incidentally, prevent the contamination of others. When a child is initiated into the faith by the Navjote ceremony the candidate must be made ready by a ritual bath,[13] but the presence of juddin friends or of lax Zoroastrians does not vitiate the ceremony. Weddings, traditionally performed in the compound of the bride's home, have, like Navjotes, attained increasing importance to a community concerned for its survival. A community compound established by a philanthropic donor has, therefore, also become a popular site for these rites because it accommodates an assembly as large as the host-family can afford to invite for the communal feast. In any case, it is not the site but the principals whose ritual purity is essential to the validity of the ritual and who, to that end, must

---

[12] Doongerwadi, the Parsis' Bombay "cemetery," is divided into areas, one for bunglis and the other for dakhmas, with a gate between Juddins may visit the bungli area subject only to the restrictions noted. Special permission, however, had to be secured from the Parsi Panchayat for the writer to pass through the gate and walk the path leading to the dakhmas—actual entrance to which was, of course, forbidden.

[13] The ritual bath is part of the *Nahn* purification ceremony. *Infra*, pp. 93ff. The officiating priest, who must have satisfied the purity requirements of his profession, is the only other person whose purity is essential to the ceremonial efficacy of the Navjote.

be guided through their *Nahn* ceremonies by priests themselves ritually clean.

Rites of Passage

The human race understood itself in earliest times as part of nature and so emphasized the values of life and tribal survival. Pre-monotheistic religions applied this perception by making the seasons of nature and the stages of human life some of their most important occasions for religious observance. Monotheistic religions have placed at the center of their ritual structures the unique historical events connected with their founding and development. The older practices, however, have been retained, howbeit with their primitive crudities refined and their material objectives somewhat overlaid by moral ends. Zoroastrianism occupies a place somewhere between extremes. The prominence of prayers addressed to the celestial beings whom, according to theology, Ahura Mazda made "lords" of creation's elements, creatures and activities perpetuates in the cultus the motif of nature and its seasons. In addition the centuries-long threat of extinction posed by the hegemonic Muslims in Iran and, in this century, by population decline in India has guaranteed the persistence of the concern to live and survive. In such circumstances, it is no wonder that the rites of passage express such concern with an intensity which no amount of stress on events of history or moral ends is likely soon to equal.

Birth is guaranteed its religious halo by Avestan and Pahlavi texts that rate children as divine blessings to parents and childlessness as heaven's curse. The practice of maintaining a ritual fire in the home of a pregnant woman was once carefully followed, but the more modern custom—unless it too is honored in the breach—is the lighting of a lamp after the fifth and seventh weeks of pregnancy. The rules of most importance are those applicable to the birth itself and to the period of the mother's confinement afterward. Pious Zoroastrians expect the room for the delivery to have been consecrated, and, after the delivery, that a light should burn for three or more days in the room of confinement as protection from evil forces.

Delivery is the clue for entry of the familiar motif of purity. The mother should remain for forty days in one room where she is isolated from others and cannot contaminate by contact the furnishings of the regular living quarters of the home. The confinement is concluded with an ordinary bath, then a ritual bath for which an officiating priest and consecrated water are required. Meanwhile, the child has been given a name, the religious significance of which is that every prayer ever said at the behest or in behalf of the person throughout a lifetime will include the mention of it.

The exigencies of modernity—economic factors, especially— have introduced laxity of observance in the case of some rules. An employed wife and mother tends merely to genuflect toward compliance with the rules of isolation, and even a housewife can do little better if neither volunteering relatives nor aides that would have to be paid from a husband's modest wages are available to serve her and the rest of the household.

Navjote

When a child is ready to talk, the first words it should be taught are the names of God and Zoroaster. Beyond that, no particularly religious objectives are associated with childhood years. The initiation ceremony, however, ends the benign neglect of religious development. Performed between the child's seventh and fifteenth years— and preferably early rather than late—Navjote has the meaning of making prayer henceforth the duty of the new member of the Zoroastrian community. The principal outward signs of this duty are the sacred shirt (*sudreh*) and thread (*kusti*) which are donned by the child for the first time in the course of the ceremony. The connection with prayer is made by the rule that the kusti is to be untied and retied before saying prayers and before the grace that precedes any meal. The objective of instilling constant awareness of Zoroastrian identity and responsibility is also served by these symbols. The sudreh with its miniature front pocket (*girehban*) just below the throat is henceforth supposed to be a permanent article of apparel, worn always except when bathing, the pocket serving meanwhile to hold symbolically each day's material achievements and good deeds. That the kusti must be untied and retied not only before praying but also upon rising in the morning, when toileting, and at bath time adds numerous other occasions for cultivating the awareness of one's Zoroastrian affiliation and duty.

The Navjote ceremony is not a long ceremony but so mandatory is it, and so rich in symbolism as well, that a journalist of the faith can describe it as "perhaps the most important event in the life of a true Zoroastrian."[14] For one thing, it is the occasion for the child's first ceremonial bath, the Nahn, previously referred to in connection with purification rites (of which more must be said shortly). It is also the first and probably only time that the person — unless it is a priestly son who will choose to be ordained a priest later—will be the exclusive object of so much congratulatory attention from priests, parents and other kinsmen, and the family's friends. Even when the family decides to participate in a collective Navjote any loss of private attention felt by the candidate has as its compensation the enhancement which magnitude lends to the solemnity and pageantry of the occasion.

The child, of course, may appreciate little of the meaning which a rite rich in symbolism is meant to convey, but understanding should deepen as the passing years present opportunities to attend Navjotes for one's juniors in age. It is then, rather than in childhood, that the Zoroastrian is most likely to learn the specific meanings of the numerous artifacts and components of the rite—the cloth, color, and cut of the sudreh, the 72 threads, the manner of weaving, the three tassels, the three knots, and the tying on of the kusti; sitting, standing, and the directions faced; a lamp and fire; rice, flowers, ghee, pomegranate grains, raisins, almonds, coconut, and money— in part, sombolizing prosperity desired for the initiate, and other- wise representing payment to the priest; the opening prayer (*Patet*), a Confession of Faith, and the central penitential prayer (*Nirang-i-kusti*), two traditional and oft repeated chants (*Ahuna Vairya* and *Ashem Vohu*),[15] the recital of the prayerful Articles of Faith, and the

---

[14]Piloo N. Jungalwalla, "The Navjote Ceremony," *Parsiana*, April-July 1975, p. 23.

[15]The Ahuna Vairya and Ashem Vohu are the first two prayers a child memorizes. The former, derived from Yasna 19, and called in abbreviated form the Ahunavar, or in a pure form the Yatha Ahu Vairyo, is variously characterized as a prayer, a sacred formula, a chant, or even a spell. The message of it is that Ahura Mazda is the spiritual Lord whose orderly and righteous will should be the example for temporal rulers, and blessed is e whose works are done as for the Lord and the benefit of those in need. So efficacious, or potent, is it presumed to be that it forms a part of virtually every litany and if other prayers are never learned, can be used as substitute for any of them. The Ashem Vohu resembles the Ahuna Vairya in message, brevity, efficacy and frequency of use. The gist of it is praise of righteousness and the promise of happiness for the person whose righteousness is the subs- tance of his piety.

final benedictions.[16] Some of this basic litany is supposed to have been memorized by the candidate, but the requirement is less strictly enforced today—at least among the Parsis—than in former times.[17]

Marriage

Though the Navjote may seem very important to the individual initiate, it is the marriage ceremony, one suspects, that the community values most among the rites of passage. The child's initiation can normally be expected, but marriage is now usually by choice and on it depends the survival of the faith as well as of the community because marriage is mainly endogamous. In Iran, the practice of endogamy is the natural consequence of minority status in a society shaped by the large Muslim majority. In India, the principle was eventually made normative in order to discourage marriage with juddins and the waning of loyalty to the faith which the mixed marriage frequently abets. The most grievous alternative to endogamy for Parsis is the marriage of a daughter to a juddin, because they hold that religious identity is inherited from the father. There is hardly a priest who will perform the ceremony, and while the wife may retain her Zoroastrian standing, neither husband nor children can be initiated into the faith. It is common in such circumstances for the wife, therefore, to grow indifferent to the faith which no amount of interest on her family's part can ever qualify them to adopt. By comparison, only celibacy comes close to a daughter's exogamy as a way of life found threatening. It offends piety because

---

[16]The Articles of Faith are the Zoroastrian equivalent of a Christian creed. The worshiper affirms belief in Ahura Mazda and praises the value of good thoughts, words, and deeds. The Mazdayasnian religion is proclaimed as the source of peace and as the best of all religions whether past or future. It ends with proclaiming God to be the source of all things good. The initiate, however, may understand very little of the texts recited, inasmuch as the versions memorized are in the Avestan and Pazand languages. (Pazand was derived from the Pahlavi language of Sasanian times by substituting words of Aryan origin for Semitic ones and employing Avestan script for writing it. It is used for short prayers supplementing the Avestan texts of Zoroastrian liturgies.)

[17]The texts that *must* be memorized are those which accompany washing with water all exposed parts of the body on every occasion of untying and retying the kusti. The ablution and recital are called *Padyab* and the whole performance a *padyab-kusti*. The necessity involved is obvious. Once the young Zoroastrian has donned the sudreh and kusti in Navjote, every day thereafter will provide its several—or—numerous occasions for padyab-kusti to be repeated.

it runs counter to the tradition derived from the *Avesta* itself that marriage and parenthood are the superior state and thus very nearly one's "religious duty,"[18] but worse, it intensifies one form of anxiety about death, especially in recent years when it has become a phenomenon common enough to exacerbate a community already worried about the effects of other demographic factors upon its capacity to survive.

Less threatening as an alternative to endogamy is the exogamous marriage of sons. *Their* children qualify for Zoroastrian initiation and so, ideally, the sons are helping to preserve the faith by reproduction. Yet anxiety remains. As in many societies, a father's interest in religion and his daily opportunities for influencing his children are less than the mother's. In consequence, the children are very likely taught their mother's religion while the father's connection with his own languishes until it is merely nominal at best. No wonder, then, that this community, concerned to survive, tends to celebrate its marriages between Zoroastrians with such visible pride and joy—not to say, relief.

Traditional practices preparatory to marriage and many of those associated with the wedding are dictated more by social custom than religious injunction. The *Avesta* and later tracts have given little guidance except where morality and ethical integrity need safeguarding. Thus marriage is to wait upon the attainment of maturity[19] and a betrothal (engagement) once made is declared hardly less binding than marriage itself. Also there have been times when priests marked engagements with minor prayerful rites. But for the most part, custom's own logic has shaped the changing patterns of habit and usage.

Today, the engagement is usually a matter of a couple's own choice rather than by parental arrangement. The day of making it official is determined by beliefs holding that certain days are auspicious. A day for the wedding is similarly determined. There are often several occasions between the two days when the families of the engaged couple call upon each other with traditional gifts

[18]Modi, *RCCP*, p. 15.

[19]Custom upstaged even the hallowed *Avesta*, however, when many Parsis adopted the Indian practice of so-called child marriage; i.e., arranging engagements for sons and daughters while they were yet children or even infants. Not until the present century did enlightened opinion and civil government bring an end to the practice.

of money, clothing, and rings, the values of which—except when families are wealthy—are more symbolic than material. Religious ceremony is not introduced until the third and second days before the wedding when deceased ancestors are honored. Finally, on the wedding day itself, the couple must prepare for the evening ceremony by taking a sacred bath, the Nahn.[20]

The home of the bride provides the setting, but when it is small, a public hall or open court available to Zoroastrians is reserved for the well-attended rite. After the Nahn, the groom appears wearing a traditional stiff hat, a light gown or robe over trousers, and holding a shawl in his hand. He is joined by the bride gowned in white and the two take seats facing each other. They are separated at first by a cloth curtain, but by several small symbolic acts that issue in tying their right hands together and removing the cloth, the notion is conveyed that union is ending their separateness. It is with these introductory formalities that explicitly religious facets of the wedding rite are first made manifest in the form of repeated recitation (in Avestan) of the sacred Ahuna Vairya formula by the officiating priests.

The central and longest portion of the ceremony begins when the bride and groom, having thrown rice at each other betokening the wish for mutual happiness and prosperity, take seats side by side, each supported by a male relative, preferably a married one, as witness. A brief invocatory blessing intoned by the senior of two priests asks of God the gifts of long life, love, many children, health, and prosperity. The witnesses are then asked if as representatives of their respective families they agree to the marriage, and the couple likewise is asked to affirm the will to marry. The assurances are sought and given three times—a guarantee, it would seem, that the marriage is the consequence of free and responsible decision-making—and thus being themselves reassured that their complicity is justified, the two priests launch into a lengthy address delivered in Pazand.

That the address is commonly referred to as a recital provides a clue to its nature. So traditional is it that it can be intoned in unison or antiphonally by the two priests who, knowing the text by rote, know also when sentence or paragraph endings provide the pauses for throwing a few grains of rice at the seated couple. The address

---

[20]*Infra,* pp. 93ff.

begins with admonitions detailing virtues to be cultivated and evils to be avoided. It is the rare Zoroastrian who knows Pazand but those who have had the gist of the admonitions described for them would, if they knew something about nineteenth century England as well, recognize the same spirit as that which informed a Victorian manual for proper young ladies and gentlemen. With the benedictions, however, any notion involving imagined outside influence is dispelled. The thirty Yazatas (angels) for whom the days of the month are named are cited for their respective attributes of character or function and held up as models for human emulation. Fidelity to Zoroastrianism and its ideals is enjoined, with reference now to exemplary kings of ancient Iran and to objects of nature associated with power or beauty. The ceremony draws to a close with benedictions once more entreating God to bestow blessings spiritual and material, this time with added emphasis upon the religion and community as the couple's co-beneficiaries.

The wedding feast and other rites of celebration and induction to married life, like their counterparts in all cultures, are gay and joyous. They are also essentially secular. If there is the appearance of uniqueness, it is because every culture evolves its own styles, its own forms of the essential artifacts of daily life, and its own ways of using these ceremonially in fashioning its rites of passage. What is distinctive about the Zoroastrian wedding, however, is that the central and most religious liturgical section of the rite as a whole is unintelligible. Zoroastrianism is alone among reasonably enlightened religions with comparably enlightened constituencies not because it uses dead languages as the media of the service but because the meaning of the texts is not in any way supplied, either by literal translation or by astute summations. To be sure, these are available, but that is different from being in circulation in easily distributed form. The lack of instructive topical publications is decried by Zoroastrians themselves, and while that lack might be remedied by priests trained to teach, preach, and counsel, the fact is that the priests are *not* so trained. It is the rare priest, indeed, who is trained, competent, or ever asked to explain the text of the wedding rite. Familiarity with it, therefore, is usually limited to having a rough notion of the content of the two brief prayers, Ahuna Vairya and Ashem Vohu, and a suspicion that the central address is recommending good thoughts, good words, good deeds—and reproduction. For some traditionalists, this is enough, since they hold that prayers correctly spoken and rites correctly performed effectively establish connection with the divine realm and generate the flow of its benefits to the aspiring petitioners. Skeptics, looking at the rising divorce rate, are not so sure. That problem, however, is better] discussed in another context.

Purification Rites

The ubiquity of concern for purity, as many times mentioned, gives rise to the thought that descriptions of how purity is achieved should be provided forthwith, as a *sine qua non* of understanding a number of rites which cannot be performed without it.

Padyab

The simplest purification rite, the Padyab,[21] would not by itself invite an inference that purity is especially prominent as a motif in thought and practice. After all, there is nothing uncommon about some form of morning ablution and periodic washing of the uncovered portions of the body in the course of a day. These actions are made distinctive, however, by sacralizing them and by retaining archaic features both to a degree hardly matched by other religions —even very traditional ones—in the present day. One example is the use of cow's urine as the cleansing agent for the first ablution of the morning.[22] Another is the repetition of a short invocatory prayer followed by the Ashem Vohu every time the Padyab is performed, to sacralize ordinary physical functions and perpetuate customs intended as reminders of religious identity and duty.

It may be, of course, that distinction inheres more in the traditional theory than in today's practice, at least for the urbanized and cosmopolitan Zoroastrians who presently constitute the great majority of believers. It is the one act of purification which a Zoroastrian, once initiated, performs without a priest's participation, and which depends, therefore, on individual conscientiousness for its observance. The recurring complaints voiced about laxity by observant traditionalists have basis in fact, for laxity is readily

[21]See n. 17.

[22]See Modi, *RCCP*, p. 93. It appears, despite some ambiguity, that Modi was saying urine is normally used only for the first ablution of the morning and that the cleansing preceding each Padyab proper thereafter during the day is usually by water. Since Modi's time, many urban Zoroastrians are said to substitute commercial antiseptics or water for the urine of the morning rite.

admitted by many Zoroastrians who say they could hardly perform all of the expected Padyabs of the day when, except for attending formal religious services and ceremonies, they have ceased even to wear the sudreh and kusti.

Nahn

The Nahn is a rite relevant to a very limited number of occasions, but an important one because of its indispensability as a prerequisite to initiation and marriage by religious ceremony. It is made indispensable by requiring a priest to officiate, and no priest will initiate or marry persons without their having "gone through" the Nahn first.

Whether performed in a home or at a fire-temple, the properties required are a stool of a hard, nonporous material, the ceremonially consecrated urine (*Nirang*) of a pure, white bull, ordinary bovine urine (*gomez*), some consecrated ash (*Bhasam*) from a fire-temple of the first (highest) grade, some sand, and a pomegranate leaf.[23]

The candidate must first do a Padyab and say the prayer that precedes a meal. Then, sitting on the stool, he receives the pomegranate leaf on a cloth so that it can be raised to the mouth untouched by the hands. Each of three sips of Nirang from a small cup is preceded by a sentence which (in translation) declares as its purpose the purification of body and soul. The prayers which follow a meal and the act of "Kusti" conclude the preliminary portion of the Nahn as a whole.

The central and purifying act of Nahn is the bath. The gomez from an ordinary bull is the first bathing agent, and the participant must retire to a bathroom for undressing. The Patet and Ashem Vohu prayers are said and a priest proceeds to hand in from the outside a spoon fastened to a long stick, followed by a sequence of vessels containing the gomez, fine sand, and consecrated water. Each of these agents is rubbed over the body three times. Finally, a more complete bath is taken with water which a few drops of the consecrated water serves also to consecrate. In redressing, the Padyab must of course be completed. New clothes sprinkled with the consecrated water are required, however, as the visible sign of having effected the desired state of purity. The closing prayers are

---

[23]The pomegranate had symbolic association in antiquity with fertility and eternal life.

no problem. They are the same as those of the numerous Padyabs of every day.

The Nahn is a prerequisite to Navjote and to marriage. In Modi's time, it was also expected for women at the close of the forty days spent in isolation following childbirth. However, the tradition of annual observance sometime during the ten days that close the Zoroastrian year has become nearly a dead letter for all except the most punctilious of the laity, and modern hygienic practices are rapidly making the Nahn after a woman's confinement also a matter of option.[24]

Bareshnum

The purification rite that is most elaborate—because intended to restore purity after exposure to the worst kinds of defilement—is the Bareshnum. Although scripturally prescribed for every Zoroastrian exposed to infection or physically communicable pollution, it would seldom be performed in modern times were it not required of candidates for the priesthood before their ordination. It also serves in the case of the already ordained priest as a guarantee of the purity requisite to his conducting the Nahn and the higher liturgical services.

Today, the Bareshnum, though still the most embellished rite of its genre, is a somewhat simplified form of the ancient rite. An outdoor rectangular space somewhere in a fire-temple compound is marked out with a nine-knotted stick by an officiating priest, and twenty-one sets of stones alternating in number of stones per set

---

[24]Zoroastrians of cosmopolitan Iranian communities uniformly testified in response to my inquiries in September, 1977 that, there, soap and water are the purifying agents for the Nahn except in remote rural regions where archaic traditionalism still obtains. In the London area, however, the senior priest (part-time) has a small quantity of Nirang in a vial that was flown to him from Bombay and which he doles out parsimoniously for sipping before Navjotes and weddings. There is some casuistry involved here. The priest steadfastly believes that consecration of the Nirang imbues it with a power to purify and bestow spiritual benefit but at the same time had violated customary rules about treating "holy things." Contact with earth had been broken by having the container flown, and observation and handling of it by non-Zoroastrians had been allowed. Dastur Kotwal of Bombay gave as his opinion, in an interview on December 9, 1977, that such Nirang would have lost its "manthric power" and could at most give "solace" to the credulous.

between three and five are placed in a line.[25]   The appropriate artifacts are brought—some already consecrated, others yet to be.
These are Nirang, consecrated ash, water, metal cups, a pomegranate leaf, and two sticks.   Two priests consecrate the water with
drops of urine and ash, and the officiating priest, having removed
his clothes, takes a ritual bath and redresses.   The final steps of
preparation have been completed when several sacred texts have
been recited and more lines have been drawn to separate the
enclosed sacred space from profane surroundings.

Now the waiting candidate prepares to enter the sacred space by
reciting prayers of grace and penitence and by partaking of the leaf
and Nirang.   He is then ready to disrobe and to sit upon the first
set of stones.   The ensuing action consists of advancing from the
first to the last of the sets of stones while performing eighteen ablutions with Nirang, eighteen with sand, and eighteen with consecrated water.   The required prayers will meanwhile have been
recited several times by the officiating priest and the candidate will
thirteen times have touched a dog brought toward him by the
assisting priest from the left side of the consecrated area.   A rinsing
of the hand after the last touching and the candidate is ready to
don new clothes.   Brief prayers, then a formula repeated three
times, asserting that the demonic Spirit, *Nasu*, and the pollution
she (!) can cause have been vanquished, and a tying of a special
ceremonial Kusti complete the rite.

It should not be assumed, however, that the candidate for purity
is ready at last to resume his normal activities or, if preparing for
the priesthood, to go on to the ordination service.   The outdoor
rite is only prelude to a nine-day period of retreat in a temple.   The
retreat is marked by the candidate's isolation, various tabus on
what may be touched, frequent recitation of prayers, avoidance of
nocturnal emissions, and outdoor ablutions with Nirang and consecrated water on the third, seventh, and tenth days.   With the
last of the baths, one Bareshnum and its obligatory retreat have
been completed.

---

[25]The sets of stones apparently vary in number according to local traditions.
Boyce reports that the sets number only nine for a Bareshnum in the rural
village of Sharifabad, Iran. See "A Last Stronghold of Traditional Zoro-
astrianism," Teaching Aid, No. 7, Bloomington, Indiana: Asian Studies Research
Institute, Indiana University, 1977. p. 27 (mimeographed, hereafter cited as
"A Last Stronghold").

The one Bareshnum in its two parts establishes the purity of a lay person or priest after defilement for any cause either imagined or real. The candidate for first ordination (Navar), however, must repeat both parts either immediately or after a few days' interval. His two periods of seclusion notwithstanding, he continues the retreat for six more days while two priests prepare themselves to share in the culminating rites. These, spread over a period of four days, engage the candidate himself in ritual performance and complete the activities requisite to his priestly conduct of Navjote, marriage, funeral, and Afringan ceremonies.[26] If he intends to perform priestly services only as avocation, the Navar ordination suffices.

The candidate for higher ordination (Martab) must complete still one more Bareshnum and, on the day following the long retreat, perform the *Khub* ceremony—i.e., recite the whole of the Yasna while performing the ritual that goes with it. He is then said to be "with the Khub," the meaning of which is that he is qualified to perform purification rites and all liturgies, both the outer ones and the high inner rites of the Yasna, Videvdat, and Baj ceremonies.[27] Martab ordination thus qualifies him in all necessary respects for making priesthood his vocation and for entering into the service of a fire-temple.

A liability of the vocation when it is full time is that duty consists so largely of ritual performance, for which a good memory is the principal qualification, that there is little time for rational reflection. Even with time, texts recited in dead languages that were studied only briefly in early adolescence can provide no provocation to indulge in fresh, creative thought. One can understand, therefore, why the priests expect still to undergo the rite of Bareshnum though it depends for its justification on archaic conceptions that confuse physical with moral and spiritual purity and that per-

---

[26]These are the so-called outer ceremonies that may be performed outside the fire-temple. An Afringan is a ceremony honoring any of the heavenly beings referred to by name in the *Avesta* and imploring blessing of either material or spiritual nature for some person living or dead. Some benefit is sought as well for the person who has requested the service. It is used in its several variant forms on the days following a death in the family, subsequent anniversary dates, and—when observed—the days of the six seasonal festivals (called *Gahambars*) of the Zoroastrian year.

[27]*Infra*, pp. 105ff.

sist because they remain unexamined. The laity may not have made
their own examination in any systematic sense, but their work-a-day
world is one demanding that common sense meanings be spread
before them—and not merely alleged—for what they are told it is
important to do. Since what is archaic has few such meanings left to
perceive, the laity can be expected to go on leaving the Bareshnum
to the priests as their preserve. That for decades the laity have
been confining observance of even the simpler Nahn to the two
occasions when the priests require it implies doubts about its relevance as well. But *it* is not, after all, an ordeal intended to prove
by difficult or painful trial one's rights or powers. Some of its
several meanings are inherently neither archaic nor irrelevant. Their
intelligent articulation by the priests might establish their relevance
and preserve the Nahn from benign neglect.

The Last Rite of Passage

The rites attendant upon death are among the outer ceremonies
the account of which was interrupted in order to explain the nature
and place of purification rites in their larger context. Now the
account may be resumed, and it is important to do so lest it be
inferred that the Zoroastrian ritual response to death is a merely
typical instance of Zoroastrian ritualism in general or of this rite
as practiced by other religions. This is not the case. It is the one
outer ceremony that in most Zoroastrian communities is not a fully
public rite. It is one of only two rites in which (as still practiced
by the Parsis in India) a dog has place, and that for a reason
which thoughtful Zoroastrians must find difficult to harmonize with
their contemporary theology. It is the one rite of its genre in the
world (or the one at least most often cited) which in most Zoroastrian communities is concluded with exposing the naked corpse to
birds of prey. Finally, it is the rite which, unlike the rites designed
for achieving purity, is most dramatically indicative of an acute
concern to ward off pollution. This degree of concern may, of
course, have been typical of Zoroastrians centuries ago and not be
a mark of their present day descendants. Nevertheless, the liturgical texts and the rubrics of those persons with roles to play when a
death occurs have the ancient Videvdat for authority, and there
the reasons are sharply etched. Moreover, the effective opposition
to all suggestions for revision except when external necessity has
required it must indicate some readiness still to be moved by consi-

derations originally conjured up in that earlier age.

The combative effort to contain infection and the spread of contamination begins shortly after death. The body is bathed with gomez and water, then clothed with a sudreh, kusti, and freshly washed garments. Two persons are supposed to attend the body and for a brief time mourners may express their affection or respect by touch or embrace if they wish. By then, professional corpse bearers (*Nasasalars*) will have arrived to shroud the body and to relieve others of any responsibility that would entail touching it.[28] In fact, no one except the bearers should be in contact with it after they have spread the shroud and positioned the body in preparation for the funeral service.

At this stage, according to tradition, *Druj-i-Nasush* (Nasu) the evil demon in league with Angra Mainyu, has begun her destructive work of making the body decay. The process cannot be prevented, but the threat to the living can be countered. The positioning of the body in a shallow sanded rectangle in the ground or on a stone slab is designed to keep contagion isolated in one place that can be cleansed later without great difficulty. The body should not face the North because the ancestral view was that manifold evils come from that direction. A metal stick or nail is used by a bearer to trace three circles around the area occupied by the body and thus create in effect an enclosure offering further deterrence to the spread of contagion. *Paiwands* (pieces of cloth or cotton tapes) serve as additional obstruction to the transmission of pollution to the living. The bearers hold a paiwand between them when they enter and while caring for the body, and all the persons who walk in the funeral procession to the dakhma do so in pairs with paiwands. That it may be comforting to people thus to demonstrate, according to Modi, their mutual readiness "to co-operate and

---

[28]The sequence so far is Modi's version in *RCCP*, pp. 54-55. It is not necessarily in contradiction with Rustomjee who says that the Nasasalars bathe and redress the corpse, for it may well be that it is the rare family that does not shy away from performing this task. Besides, the custom of caring for the deceased and holding the funeral rites at home has waned. The dead are transported as quickly as possible to special houses in residential areas or, in cities like Bombay, bunglis built on the same grounds as the corpse-exposure towers (dakhmas), where it would be natural for the bearers to assume all the duties preliminary to the funeral rites. See Framroz Rustomjee, "Zoroastrian Ceremonies for the Disposal of the Dead," a pamphlet (2nd ed.; Colombo: The Nadaraja Press, 1964), pp. 2, 3.

sympathise with each other,"[29] is a reasonable explanation of the paiwand, but it seems suspiciously too reasonable to account for a practice so strictly adhered to in India. An alternative explanation is that the paiwand attracts the forces of defilement and localizes them in its center, whereas individual (unpaired) persons in attendance would be unable to deflect the flow of evil forces traveling directly toward their hearts.[30]

Another unusual practice, called *sagdid*, is that of having a dog view the corpse, twice during the shrouding, again at the beginning of each gah that passes before all rites are concluded, once at the close of the liturgical service, and finally just before the body is borne into the dakhma.[31] Once more, rational speculation conjures up a variety of possible reasons for the several sagdids, with priority given to the notion that the dog will stare steadily at the body if all life is gone from it and thus prevent bearing a person still living into the dakhma. The Videvdat's reason, however, is usually ignored. The four-eyed dog, so this text declares, frightens away the "corpse demon," Nasu.[32]

The liturgy begins with prayer, the *Sraosh-baj*, asking Sraosha's protection against evil. It is recited by the bearers, one portion before bathing and clothing the corpse, the remainder when they have finished. Two priests then perform the central *Geh-Sarna* ceremony, the recitation of the Ahunavaiti Gatha (Yasna XXVIII-XXXIV).

Where tradition still rules, priests normally will not officiate unless juddins, calling to pay their respects, withdraw to positions which will not permit them to see the corpse once the bearers are ready to bathe it. Only Zoroastrians may attend the service, and only the men, dressed in white, and after reciting part of the Sraosh-baj, follow the bearers in paiwand-joined pairs to the dakhma. When the bearers have carried the corpse inside and, by removing its clothes, disclosed it to vultures, the waiting mourners take the bearers' return as the cue for completing their Sraosh-baj. A gomez and water ablution is necessary before leaving the site, and an

[29]Modi, *RCCP*, p. 55. The same explanation is given again on p. 64.

[30]Dabu, *Hand-Book*, pp. 43, 44.

[31]The dog is supposed to have two light spots above the eyes, which explains why the animal is referred to as a four-eyed dog. If no dog with such marks is readily available, however, any dog will do.

[32]Videvdat 3:14.

ordinary bath upon reaching home is customary practice for everyone who attended any part of the service in any capacity.

The rites so far described are those which treat of the mortal body
and for which the time allotted is not to exceed twenty-four hours.
The soul, however, is believed to remain on earth for three days
under the protection of Sraosha, and so it is to the soul's welfare
that the mourning kinsmen turn their attention after the funeral.
With the aid of at least two priests invited to the home, the relatives mark the beginning of every gah throughout the three days
with the recitation of a Sraosh-baj, the prayers regularly associated
with each gah, and the Patet prayer of penitence.   The rite of each
evening's gah is ceremonially the most important.   Called an
Afringan (i.e., a service of praise), it requires a fire, pure water, and
flowers specially arranged.   The conscientious family will also wish
that the inner ceremony of the Yasna and other rites at a fire-
temple be dedicated to the deceased during this three-day period.
If there are charities to which commemorative donations are to be
directed, announcement of these is made at the rite for the after-
noon gah of the third day when, by reason of the addition of
prayers for the deceased and the attendance, again, of friends, the
rite is called an *Uthamna*.

The last and most solemn of the post-funeral series of rites, held
at dawn of the fourth day, *Cheharum*, centers concern upon the soul
of the deceased as it takes its leave of earth.   The pattern of the
Uthamna is repeated, for Sraosha's continuing protective care is
needed, still, for the soul's journey to Chinvat, the bridge of judgement.   Traditional belief holds that the soul's prototypal Fravashi,
also, accompanies it, guarding and guiding it as it has done on earth.

The Fravashi thereafter remains the link between the departed
soul and those surviving who cherish their memories of the deceased.
Subsequent Afringan ceremonies, therefore, invoke the Fravashi and
serve the purposes of sustaining remembrance and of maintaining
a relationship of reciprocal helpfulness between the living and the
dead.   The tenth day, the thirtieth day, a year after death, and then
annually (for as long as there are living descendants who had
acquaintance with the deceased) are the proper times for these continuing observances.[33]   Selective omissions, however, are not un-

---

[33]See Modi, *RCCP*; pp. 78-86 for explanations of post-funeral rites, and 377-
407 for a description of Afringan memorial ceremonies, especially those
held annually on the last days of the religious year.

common in the present day when it may not be as easy to compen-
sate the priests in cash as it once was with goods, and when, moreover, the structures of modern life give most Zoroastrians other
things to think about than ancestors' souls or currying favors for
them from ministering angels.

A number of other deviations from tradition have been adopted
by Zoroastrians in lands where ancient practices would be quite
unfamiliar, not to say strange. The communities formed by migration to the West have uniformly adopted such locally prevailing
conventions as dependence upon "secular" morticians, cemetery
burial or cremation of the body, unrestricted attendance at all the
funeral rites, and freedom qualified only by what is reasonably good
taste in such matters as dress, personal hygiene, and deportment in
general. In Iran also, most distinctively Zoroastrian cultic practices
have been all but abandoned. Hardly anyone knows what a paiw-
and is; restrictions and tabus for the sake of protecting Zoroastrians
from juddins are treated as archaic; and dakhmas survive, if at all,
only as vestiges of the past except for a few possibly still occasion-
ally used in remote villages.[34] The memorial rites of the several
days after a funeral and on anniversary dates are retained, but the
mythopoeic notions that they are vehicles for co-opting benevolent
heavenly powers and gaining their support for the soul in its ascent
to judgment are no longer taught. The unchanged ritual texts of a
post-Gathic age contain these notions, of course, but translating
them in order to transmit their ideas is not a present-day concern.
The reason given today for memorial rites is the simpler and easily
understood one of holding in affectionate regard those forbears
upon whom dependence is acknowledged for one's own life and
heritage.[35] Even on traditional Parsi soil the laity are abetting the

---

[34]Although already aware of the accommodation made to Western funeral
practices by Zoroastrians in England and America, I was both surprised and—
as I saw it—honored when invited by officers of the Tehran Zoroastrian
Anjuman to participate in the funeral and burial rites held for one of the
members of the community on the grounds of their cemetery outside the city.
There, in Zoroastrians' native Iran, I was urged to ask any questions I wished
and shown every courtesy that was extended to intimates of the deceased.
Similar freedom to enter fire-temples and participate in rites like any behdin of
the faith was experienced in Shiraz and even the old and in many ways still
traditional town of Yazd.

[35]This is not to say there are no remnants of ancient thought still quite well
understood and cherished by villagers whose traditions have not yet had a

same trend. Priests may have their professional motives for holding
to the idea that the welfare of ancestral souls is in some indispensable way determined by the rites which their descendants commission in their behalf; but the idea is hardly consistent with the time-
honored view that a person's eternal destiny is shaped in the last
analysis by his own thoughts, words, and deeds.   Latter-day Parsis
as well as Zoroastrians in general are inclined to think that prayers,
too, affect the quality of life for the quick, not the dead.

Seasonal and Other Rites
Gahambars

Associated with the religion for the greater part of its history,
festivals called Gahambars have given Zoroastrians periodic respite
from labor and occasions to give thanks for earthly blessings.   Six
seasonal times were designated, each correlated with a phase of
agricultural production and one of them with the year-end *Muktad*
holidays as well.   The period of a gahambar is five days, but the
fifth day is the only one given over to celebration; the other four
are for preparation and anticipation of the fifth day's feasting.   The
social unit composing the gathering may be a family or a neighbour-
hood.   Of course liturgical rites precede the feasting. Two of these
are outer   ceremonies.   The appropriate inner ceremony is the
Visparad rite, but it is optional.

The high priority that Gahambars held among the religious ceremonies for centuries on end has been lost, however, except in rural
communities where daily life and cultural patterns are still agrarian
and flexible.   Now that most Zoroastrians are minorities dwelling
in urban centers, the activities engaged in at home and at work are
not those that can be fully and frequently interrupted for days at a
time.   In any case, urban daily life itself seldom requires the dawn
to dusk labor that generates the need for numerous lengthy re-

---

serious "brush" with modernity. The notions of the Zoroastrians of Sharifabad, where Boyce spent seven months in field work, agree essentially as she
dscribes them with the traditional views about death, souls, and ancestors
explained by Modi. Her ascription of these, however, to Zoroaster himself,
and the repect she seems to accord them on that account, are the consequences—said *my* informants, urbanely—of having been instructed by a "pagan
priest" who did not discriminate between the ideas of the prophet and the
veneer of primitive conceptions which have been re-associated with them. See
Boyce, "A Last Stronghold," pp. 14-20.

prieves. If, therefore, the "passing" of the Gahambars is felt as loss, the regret arises chiefly among the priests, for the rites which generate gifts and fees are accordingly diminished.

Muktad Ceremonies

Known also by an older name, *Fravardegan*, the Muktad holidays are the last ten days of the religious year. The older term is Iranian and points more explicitly than does the somewhat obscure 'Muktad' to their purpose, that of honoring Fravashis. As Modi explained, speaking plainly, "They are the principal holy days for the remembrance of the dead."[36] At this point, it may be recalled that the last five days of the ten are the sixth group of Gahambar holidays as well. This has guaranteed that Gahambars would not be honored entirely in the breach. Also, because Pahlavi writings imputed an added cosmogonic meaning to each Gahambar period— in the case of the sixth, rejoicing in the creation of the human race—the Muktad's meanings have reference to life as well as to death, for mingled with "memory for the dead" is "hope for our future."[37]

The essential rites are those performed in homes, the nearest descendants of persons recently deceased taking turns from year to year as hosts. A raised stand is placed in a hospitable room to hold flowers, water for their vases, and offerings of fruit. The daily ritual is usually held in the evening when it is most convenient for relatives to gather, during which time at least, a fire of candalwood is kept burning. Since the principal liturgical texts for these daily rites come from Pazand and portions of the *Avesta* which none of the laity know, priests find their services in greater demand than at any other time of the year, the more so if some families can afford to pay also for the daily recital of inner ceremonies at a fire-temple. The laity are not thereby relieved of ritual duty, for they are expected to do recitations from the Yasna, especially the Gathas. If they do not know these passages, however, the familiar Ashem Vohu and

---

[36]Modi, *RCCP*, p. 465.

[37]*Ibid.*, p. 471. Modi's sentiment would be regarded as more sanguine than accurate by reformers among the Parsis. It is a common complaint that the priests and lay traditionalists do nothing to make religion a "living force," enhancing to "happiness and prosperity," but "let it be [instead] a spent force in the service of the dead who are dead." Dara J.D. Cama, *We Parsis, Our Prophet, and Our Priests*, (Bombay, 1966), p. 18.

Ahuna Vairya prayers may be repeated over and over as substitutes.

In the newer Western settlements, the daily rites may be held at a Setayashgah (house of prayer) and on a community rather than merely kinship basis. Such is the case in London, for example, where several men with priestly qualifications voluntarily take turns by twos in chanting the texts appropriate to the several evenings' rites. It is also common on such occasions for earnest behdins to follow the progress of the recitations from books containing English transliterations and to join *sotto voce* in saying the prayers familiar to them. The simplest of observances may still find place in homes, but the community services become the important ones. These can be quite lengthy, however, inasmuch as the Muktad recitations must include calling the names of all the deceased persons whose families have asked for them; on a community-wide basis, the list can be a long one.

Jashans

The celebrations known by this term include those of the Gahambars and Muktad and of many other times or occasions as well. The utility of the term is probably explained by its kinship with words meaning praise or worship. In any case, the celebration of almost any gratefully recalled event by engaging in worship and fasting may be called a Jashan. The Jashans mentioned so far are mainly those spread over several days and having either seasons or ancestors as their *raison d'etre*. Another sub-species consists of those that fall on that day of each month which bears the name of that month itself. These are for honoring the divinities who individually or as a group are associated, each in turn, with a given month of the year. Still other Jashans commemorate by a single rite on a single day some blessing of nature or a season, an event hallowed by a community, or some more broadly historical occasion of national import. Such examples as New Year's Day, Zoroaster's date of birth, the boons of fire and water, the anniversary of the founding of a fire-temple, and the establishment of peace after war suggest the wide range of reasons there can be for these thanksgiving celebrations.[38]

---

[38]See Moulton's concise and interpretive references to the Jashans, in *The Treasure of the Magi*, pp. 168, 169.

That there are expenses for such festivities is a foregone conclusion, but these, like the construction costs of fire-temples, have often been met by philanthropists who designated trust funds for underwriting the feasts and the services of the priests.[39] Not even free admission for the guests, however, has sustained the one-time popularity of anything like the number of holidays which the interests and money of willing donors added to the calendar with the passage of the years. The available income from the funds may still be fully used in the few intimate and traditional communities that remain, but not a few of the bequests in the increasingly cosmopolitan centers either accumulate to no good purpose or must have their charitable objectives re-defined by appeal of the trustees to the courts.

The Baj and Afringan Ceremonies

The novice in Zoroastrian studies is often confused by the number of terms which seem to be used interchangeably for a common phenomenon. References to the Bajs and to Afringans, Jashans, and Gahambars in the same context provide a case in point. The confusion is not without warrant; some components of a liturgical rite may be parts of many other rites, purposes may be overlapping, and a genre of holidays may be one of several types within a larger whole.

The confusion diminishes when it is realized that terms such as 'Jashan' and 'Gahambar' refer to *occasions*, while 'Baj' and 'Afringan' denote two principal kinds of *liturgical rites* which, with numerous variations, are appropriate to those occasions. 'Jashan' is a broadly inclusive term because it is any "important . . . occasion, whether joyful or melancholy"[40] that is celebrated in part by a service of worship. Gahambars are thus but one of several genres of Jashans.

As regards the ceremonies, 'Afringan' denotes a less comprehensive genre than does 'Baj'. Both are classified as outer ceremonies because almost all of them may be performed outside a fire-temple, but an Afringan is distinguished by the fact that its prime objective is always the welfare of persons. The prayers recited honor the

---

[39]The cost of Jashans has also been met by inviting subscriptions from would-be participants or by grants from the treasury of a sponsoring committee. See reference to Bombay's Jashan Committee, *supra*, pp. 64-65.

[40]Modi, *RCCP*, p. 64-65.

deities and then seek blessing from them for either the dead or the living and for the person who has requested the rite. The rubric for a given Afringan dictates, on the bases of the day, season, and purpose of performance, the passages to use from the Yasna, the Yashts, or (probably most often) the Khordeh Avesta, the "Zoroastrian Prayer Book." Some Afringans can be recited on any day. Others are designated for use, principally, on particular days related to the time of a person's death, for Gahambars, and one of the final days of a Navar candidate's initiation process. The artifacts which the Afringans employ are further distinguishing marks. While they share two of these with most Zoroastrian rites—water, and of course the fire with sandalwood and frankincense to sustain it—they differ from Bajs in requiring trays of fruits and flowers, milk, wine, and a sweet juice (in small vessels).

The texts and the edible items bear their testimony to the fact that the rite is a sacrificial meal. Offered symbolically to the deities and the fravashis of the dead, it is partaken of by the living worshippers in attendance in small ceremonial amounts, the whole rite thus becoming a means of uniting those of heaven and those of earth in "blessed, sweet communion."

The problem posed by the term 'Baj' is that it has several significations all but one of which it seems to the uninitiated should be expressed by other terms.

The one Baj rite which might be described as a complete liturgical service is that which is most often performed on the fourth day after a person's death, on the monthly anniversaries during the first year thereafter,[41] and then on the yearly anniversaries. The reason for not calling it an Afringan is principally that its textual content differs, being based with only slight variations from Baj to Baj on chapters three through eight of the Yasna. Another difference is that this form of Baj, because of being restricted in its reference mainly

---

[41]The Baj of the fourth day after death becomes by repetition *four* Bajs dedicated to different yazatas and the fravashis. The number of subsequent monthly observances now varies considerably; any one or all of those that could be held between the first month's and the first year's anniversary date are frequently omitted. While their cost is an important factor, new ideas must also be taken into account. The inclination of contemporary Zoroastrians is to doubt that respect for the dead need be demonstrated by the number of rites commissioned or that the departed souls are, really, in any way benefitted by them.

to certain of death's anniversary dates or other seasonal dates, is appropriate only on certain days, whereas the Afringan services that may be performed on those same days are but a few of the many Afringans for other purposes that may be requested of the priests for any day whatever.

'Baj' refers, secondly, to the offerings that are made as a *part* of the Baj ceremony. The Afringan's flowers, wine, and fruits are replaced by several round unleavened sacred breads, pomegranate seeds, and animal products, usually ghee or butter and an egg.

So far, understanding need not be difficult of attainment. But then we find that a curious way of "muttering" Pazand prayers "in a suppressed tone" when they are interpolations between portions of prayers in Avestan is called "reciting in Baj."[42] And finally 'Baj' refers to a whole class of prayers associated mainly with common-place activities of daily life. They are simply the spoken parts of the personal "mini-rituals" already described as the purificatory Padyabs performed in the course of taking meals, toileting, and bathing. For the behdins, "taking the Baj" before the activity and "giving up, or finishing, the Baj" at its conclusion consists of reciting the texts which have provided Zoroastrians with their simplest time-honored prayers. For the priests, however, or at least for those who observe the rules that qualify them to perform all the inner ceremonies, the texts are of greater length and are more times repeated—and not just before eating but even before drinking.

The Bajs obviously have served historically as a principal mechanism for sacralizing the Zoroastrian behdin's daily life. Present practice, however, is increasingly lax. One or two of the small Bajs, like the Padyabs which they begin and end, are more likely than not the perfunctory symbols only of the many daily repetitions which were convenient in times when life's activities were home-centered for all but are not now. The priests almost alone, because the cultus *is* their *life*, perpetuate custom. At least it must be supposed that they do, for if they do not, it is a secret they are not disposed to tell.

The Priests' Preserves

The private and domestic rites which sacralize daily life and are in theory every Zoroastrian's duty to perform are numerous but

[42]Modi, *RCCP*, pp. 269, 357, 358, 373.

brief, opaque in many a detail but understood as to general purpose, often annoyingly inconvenient but inexpensive to afford. By any definition they are participatory.

The rites of passage also assume attendance. For while priests are *sine qua non* to these, the persons who are their *raison d'etre* have their own parts to play even if that means little more than being present. These take longer than domestic rites, are more costly, and have for their textual rubric archaic languages entirely unintelligible to all except the rare scholar, yet for all of that are not about to be neglected.

Time was when the same could be said for other portions of a cultus spread over and through the Zoroastrians' year. One class of rites, however, has ever been either the priests' private business or at the least, in some instances, is not held to be dependent upon behdin attendance for effect.

Paragna

Typical of this class is the *paragna* ritual required as preparation for all exclusively inner ceremonies (i.e., for the Yasna, Visparad, and Vendidad services). Inasmuch as the Yasna is supposed to be—and in every Atash Behram and most Atash Adarans, is—a daily service, the paragna too becomes a daily necessity. And it has its own cultic prerequisites. The priests have first to establish their personal bodily purity and that of their garments as part and parcel of the ritual purity (holiness) which qualifies them. They must even "clean their nails" we learn from Modi, and "have a clean mouth, so that there lurk no particles of any food between their teeth."[43]

The skeletal structure of the rite consists of gathering the items to be consecrated for later use in the Yasna ceremony. Wearing *ijar* (tight trousers) and a *padan* (cloth for covering nose and mouth) a priest makes several visits to the fire-temple's compound to collect well water, a date-palm leaf, a pomegranate twig, and milk from an unblemished goat. These, together with the various vessels, metal wires, strands of hair from a perfect white bull, and haoma twigs, are to be purified by ritual actions and consecrated by simultaneous recitation of the traditionally prescribed Avestan texts. The initial objective is to achieve ritual purity for things only physically clean at first and to raise them then from the level of ritual purity to the

[43]*Ibid.*, p. 266.

highest level, pure holiness. The second or more central objective is to establish the efficacy of the Yasna, Visparad, and Vendidad liturgies which employ these consecrated items so that they will bring "pleasure and benefit to all holy beings in the *menog* [spiritual] realm and their blessings to the *getig* [worldly] realm."[44]

Kotwal and Boyd are at pains to point out, in their detailed description of the paragna, that the righteousness of the priest's intention is as "integral to the efficacy of the ritual" as is his physical purity. Without such intent, righteousness would fail to characterize his mind, speech, and action. Yet, the substance of just what righteousness is seems illusive. The priest, they say, "must recite the holy words with utter devotion and attentiveness."[45] It is thus the sound of the Avestan words when pronounced correctly, and not conceptual understanding of them, that possesses a metaphysical correspondence with the divine realm. In fact, "proper recital of the Avesta prohibits thinking . . . in a language comprehensible to oneself."[46] Efficacy also involves associating the right ritual gestures with the chanted sounds. The actions combine with the sounds to generate power capable on the one hand of binding Angra Mainyu and his demons and, on the other, of "conveying the offering [of consecrated items] to the *menog* realm and receiving *menog* blessings."[47]

Some conception of what righteousness means can now be discerned. It means, in the case of the priest, punctilious correctness in performance. For priest and behdin alike, it means also a steadfast, reverential, credulous trust that rituals please the divinities and evoke their response in the form of various life-giving benefits.

The paragna by itself is only preliminary to this end, since it merely consecrates the items to be offered afterward in the Yasna or other inner ceremonies. It is therefore, essentially, the priests' "preserve" in the sense that it is not a service for worshipping behdins to attend. Nor are the Yasna or Visparad rites very different. Aside from the fact that they emphasize recitation more than gestures, they differ from the paragna mainly in that the consecrated offerings are finally shared, in small sips and morsels, by the performing priests and any observing behdins if present. But the pre-

[44]Firoze M. Kotwal and James W. Boyd, "The Zoroastrian *paragna* ritual." *Journal of Mithraic Studies*, II, No. 1 (1977), p. 37.

[45]*Ibid.*, pp. 36 and 38.

[46]*Ibid.*, p. 38.

[47]*Ibid.*, pp. 39 and 40.

sence of lay worshipers is not essential to efficacy here, either. Piety
may be reinforced, but the real, intended benefit of the service is so
to bring "pleasure to the *yazads* [yazatas]" that, strengthened, "they
may continue to promote the common good of mankind with their
blessings."[48] Impious though it may be, it is also logical to draw the
conclusion that such an aim requires only two surviving Zoroastrian
priests performing a daily Yasna in only one fire-temple in the
world, and all humanity can rest secure. And though no such
thought would ever be uttered, it is surely just such an unconscious
notion that prompts behdins to commission and pay the fees for
rites they do not themselves attend.

Nirangdin

A rite which is again strictly priestly business but certainly not a
daily one is that which makes consecrated nirang of the gomez
(urine) of a pure white, uncastrated bull. The procedure as a whole
is a lengthy one. The two priests who are required must prepare
themselves by the ten-day Bareshnum, and pass all the nights of it
without "nocturnal pollution." The *Gewra* of vigil and ceremonies
adds another six days to the preparation period (as in the case also
of candidacy for ordination).

The bull, himself a rather fastidiously cared-for beast, is brought
into the fire-temple where a previously cleansed metal pot awaits the
emission. The quantity is increased by adding urine from other
ordinary bulls, since it is held that the white bull's urine effectively
upgrades the others'. Another pot is filled with water from the fire-
temple's well. The collection having been completed before sunset,
and a paragna having been performed sometime during the after-
noon, the priests wait until midnight when they finally perform the
Vendidad (Videvdat). The recitation and ritual action, taking about
seven hours, achieves by consecration the highest of the three
degrees of purity for the nirang and the water—holiness or holy
purity. From it will be drawn, as long as it lasts, the small precious
amounts needed for other purification rites, such as Bareshnums
and especially the Nahns required for Navjotes and weddings.

Leaving out of account such consecrating rites as the one-time
dedication ceremonies for new fire-temples or new dakhmas and
their respective rites, the Nirangdin is altogether probably the most

---

[48]*Ibid*., p. 42

lengthy of all the repeatable rituals. It is also the single most expensive one when the cost of owning and caring for the bull is added to the value of the time spent by the priests who obviously cannot be earning fees for other services to behdins during the seventeen days they must set aside for this one.[49]

To the priests and the orthodox, of course, the cost is not to be counted in economic terms but in the value of the nirang's life-sustaining potencies. "Without nirang the [Zoroastrian] community could not survive," is one earnest priest's contention, "because it wards off evil influences, rendering them powerless to alter the good vibrations of each person's true aura."[50] But cost is not a principal reason for the spread of a quite contrary view either. Rather, it is skepticism, the increase of which with respect to issues of this kind is again the consequence of the Zoroastrians' rural-to-urban population shift and of the still more recent waves of migration to lands distant from either Iran or India. The products of the dairy barn may be useful, but urban dwellers are bound to doubt sooner or later that certain ones were divinely ordained to bear a self-evident, affinitive relationship to righteousness. For this and other reasons, the rites which the priests have preserved most intact because they are their own domain are also the ones suffering most the effects of declining credibility and reduced support.

The cultus has long been the aspect of Zoroastrianism that has given its other features their shape and character. Despite the

---

[49]Estimates of the cost of one Nirangdin, suggested by priestly informants, ran from Rs. 5,000 to Rs. 6,000 at a time in the 1970's when that would exchange for about $600 to $700. This explains why the supply of nirang is measured for use with conscientious frugality and its replenishment afforded, according to estimate, only three or four times a year by any one fire-temple. The cost would be still greater if every fire-temple had a white bull. Instead, the several fire-temples of a community or panthak share in maintaining one, sheltering it within the compound of a fire-temple with ample grounds.

[50]Zal Sethna in interview, London, August 22, 1977. By vocation an accountant, Sethna was trained and ordained a priest in India. He is one of several members of the Greater London Association who serve avocationally, by performing outer ceremonies. The "aura" is a kind of personal magnetic field around the human body which many Zoroastrians (especially those sympathetic to the ideas of Ilm-e-Khshnoom) believe projects strong currents that influence one's environment for good or ill. As compared with the average person, one who is purified by nirang, according to this view, emanates an aura of much greater potency for good.

changes that time and shifting circumstances were bound to force, much of the imposing bulk of cultic structure shows still its Magian lineage. Resistant to change itself, the religion as a whole is also.

Of course, that could hardly be said of the cultus as an impersonal phenomenon. The characterization, in other words, really describes the priests. Theirs is the only hereditary class of Zoroastrians. They have transmitted the substance and the rules from memory and by rote to such of their sons as were unresisting, each in turn being inducted into the profession and so preoccupied by its duties that those who could have developed critical faculties have seldom done so. Nor could mature behdins of thoughtful mind and constructive purpose, excluded from the profession, serve the cause of renewal.

Accorded the prestige which in earlier times people granted those who had the ear of the gods, the priests were privileged to do as they pleased—which was to devise a rite for everything and add embellishments. The work of memorizing texts and ritual gestures, and of performing repetitiously what they had memorized, precluded the critical thought and creative construction that would have resulted in theological development and the emergence of viable institutional structures enlisting the talents of the laity. Typical of the general paralysis is the impossibility of effecting liturgical revisions that would use the ancient texts in translation. The priests need only to do nothing, and so nothing *can* be done. Not that they haven't reasons. In this instance, an historian of the religion has said "they know the liturgies in translation wouldn't make sense and the behdins would find it out. As they stand, the texts' only value is as mantras, which 'work' as long as one thinks they do."[51]

One may conjecture, after observing the popularity of Navjotes and weddings, that the surviving measure of vitality still found in the cultus resides in the rites of passage. These, after all, have to do with the real life of real persons, as do also such ceremonies as those marking ordinations and deaths. If by careful observation and analy-

[51]The historian who made this remark in August, 1977, shall be nameless because it is one whose continuing labors should not be jeopardized by alienating informants. Known for entertaining respect for Zoroastrian fidelity to traditionalism if a community's whole cultural context has remained traditional, the author may prefer to leave it that way and not be regarded also as a sharp critic of what in the present day and in other contexts are anachronisms.

sis, the vitalizing features of these rites can be discerned and their anachronisms, if any, pruned away, lessons may be learned which, applied, could lead to general cultic renewal, the central purpose of which should be the daily nurture of the human spirit.

CHAPTER 5

Morality, Ethics, and Social Policy

Zoroaster as Moral Theologian

Prophetic vision is not a gift dropped from the sky to be picked up by the first person who happens by. It is the product, rather, of careful observation of life in community and of agonizing appraisal of the thought and pursuits which contribute to life's increase or its destruction. It was Zoroaster's perception that the society of his time and place was choosing destruction. Seeing in the natural order a divine creation intended to be life-giving, he took it as a model for reshaping the society, that it might be the ordered and life-supportive one he envisioned.

Earth is good, Zoroaster thought. Its soil brings forth the fruits which sustain all living creatures. Its waters cleanse and refresh. Fire gives light and warmth. All things should work together for good. But they did not. Lawless nomads preyed upon the herds and flocks of the industrious and neighbour-regarding herders. Profligate sacrifices were made to please and appease deities presumably as debauched as their worshippers, though it was human avarice and irresponsible self-indulgence that spawned the prodigality of the daeva worshippers which rendered life precarious for all.

All was of-a-piece. Religion itself was despoiled by the corruption of its practitioners, so that it became an accomplice in degrading the life it should ennoble. Men lived by lies and deceit. Their vocation was robbery; their means violence. Compacts were made only to be broken. All the good creations were exploited and wasted in "riotous living." It would never suffice to reform theology alone, or merely the sacrificial cult either. The reformation must be a radically moral one as well. The ideal for the human mind could be nothing less than Vohu Manah, the good mind of Ahura Mazda, that it might be devoted to truth (asha), constant in faithfulness, and solicitous for the welfare of all creation,

We do not find in the Gathas, of course, a thoroughly detailed moral code for personal guidance or a systematic ethic for life in society. The lineaments are there, however, for the conscientious of Zoroaster's followers to apply to the problems of their own unfolding times. With regard to commitment, Zoroaster was a perfectionist. We are given free will, the first exercise of which is to choose whom we will serve. We may choose Ahura Mazda and his righteousness or the false deavas and their lies. To err in action is only human, but there is no excuse for error in choosing which "side" we are on. The perfect choice leads to action which, even if not always perfect, is idealistic. Inspired by Ahura Mazda's own "good thoughts, good words and good deeds" (Yasna 45 : 8),[1] every person's first concern should be that his own character be one of scrupulous honesty, rectitude, trustworthiness—in sum, one of unassailable integrity.

The action of the person of character should take the form of industry, the nurture of plants, animals, and all of earth's sustaining resources, and social justice. The foundations of social peace and the common good were good stewardship and respect for other persons' rights to the fruits of their labor. Already, with Zoroaster, the outline of an ecological ethic was being sketched, millennia before the world at large would be driven by extremity to share (unwittingly) his concern. The name for the ethic as a whole is prudence, the way of moderation.

Finally, the ideal of personal integrity and the ethic of practical responsibility were perceived by Zoroaster as integrally related to worship. Choosing the right goals of life issued in a critique of both the form and the substance of the cultus. The wanton waste and cruel slaughter of useful animals for pleasing and appeasing deities, who could be only false ones if they wanted such offerings, was scandalous. Such sacrifices did not honour God; they mocked him. The intemperance of the oblations of haoma led not to spiritual ecstasy or wise discernment of the ways of God but to spiritual debasement and minds disordered by intoxication.

How much of the primitive cultus Zoroaster swept away or reinterpreted or replaced with something else will probably never be known. If, as Schmidt has advised, the strong possibility that Zoroaster's terms of pastoral life were meant as metaphors should

---

[1]Taraporewala's translation, in *The Religion of Zarathushtra*, p. 122.

discourage the thought that his Gathas contain the specific features of a "socio-economic revolution,"[2] then the idea that the precise details of how he may have reformed the cultus can be discerned must also be held suspect. At the same time, an imagery which uses good husbandry to point to proper regard for true religion implies something about the culture, and a prophet so preoccupied with discerning truth and propagating its spread cannot have been blithely uncritical of worship calculated merely to manipulate higher powers for materialistic ends by mechanical rites. The Gathas clearly show him stressing, in prayerful reflection, the soul's deep searching for the knowledge of God and God's will for man. If for him this was central to worship, Boyce is right in crediting him with adding the dimension of "ethical purpose" to ritualism, so that "the cult grew more inward and spiritual."[3] But her confidence that he inherited and then perpetuated the liturgical rubric of his time with little change except this added "dimension" is neither well supported nor really credible. A person who found himself as much alone in his aspirations as Zoroaster did would hardly have supposed that he could persuade anyone to accept new meanings for worship if he permitted the liturgical framework to remain the same as for worship of the daevas. If he did, he has been undeservedly called a prophet! If the ritual forms of later times were essentially those which he inherited, the likelihood is not that they survived because he was content merely to invest the cultus with new meaning but that he had disciples of his own stature to preserve his alterations of its form.

Granted that appearances,[4] however, cannot be inflated into probabilities, or probablities into certainties, what can be said without fear of challenge is that Zoroaster's conception of the good life went beyond affecting human behaviour; it implied an eschatology.

It is often said that virtue is its own reward. Zoroaster would not

[2]Harrs-Peter Schmidt, "Zarathustra's Religion and His Pastoral Imagery," reprint of lecture at the University of Leiden, June 1975, p. 1.

[3]Boyce, *History* I, p. 220 and *BSOAS*, XXXIII, Part I, p. 29.

[4]If one reads Boyce at some length—her *History* I (1975) will do nicely—her pattern for reconstructing ancient history becomes awe inspiring. The assurance afforded by certainty thrives and the need of solid documentation vanishes after repeating enough times, it "appears," "apparently," "it seems," "seemingly," "it would appear," "probably," 'and so forth. This is not to say that she ignores evidence. She uses it to good effect when there is some.

have agreed. Given the fierce enmity he encountered from the Druj-inspired daeva worshippers, he was painfully aware that righteousness bore not only the good fruit of a clear conscience but also the bitter fruit of unmerited suffering. He was convinced, therefore, that God was truly good only if he guaranteed to the righteous the redress of the balance in another world. Hence the doctrine that, those who, having chosen aright, so live that their good thoughts, words, and deeds outnumber the bad will have eternal place in God's kingdom and share in the final triumph of righteousness. The notion that there is some kind of existence beyond death was not new in ancient Iran. Zoroaster's originality consisted in completely reconceiving it. It must be deserved by reason of good moral character and ethical conduct. And the prize must be consonant in its nature with the effort of winning it: an eternity of bliss in the House of Song.

The Standards of the Later Avesta

The reader of the Later Avestan (post-Gathic) texts finds that Zoroaster's lofty ideals continued to be held in high regard. Truthfulness and fidelity to commitments, diligence in laboring at one's occupation, wholesome regard for nature, including sexuality, and early marriage and parenthood were principal virtues still, while lying, deceit, laziness, and asceticism were with equal zeal to be shunned.

There would arise, however, the problem of preserving such ideals without effective help from the very literature which voiced them. Both the Gathic and the Later Avestan were archaic languages by the time they came to be regarded as "Scriptural" and therefore sacred, and, later traditions to the contrary, there is no evidence that they were anything but oral until the Sasanian period.[5] This would have its own consequences. Meanwhile, the problem was that the post-Gathic material so scattered its genuflections to Zoroastrian virtues among lists of approved but trivial cultural idiosyncrasies that it is only a miracle that the texts which honored them survived until recorded. The mixture sufficed to put the

---

[5]See. R. Ghirshman, *Iran* (Penguin Books, edition of 1954), p. 318, where the *Avesta* is characterized as "a collection of oral traditions, some of them very ancient." "It remains an open question," he says, as to whether they were compiled [committed to writing] in the fourth century or as late as the sixth (A.D.).

righteousness of the ethical life into competition with a righteousness that consisted of little more than punctilious correctness in the repetitious performance of rituals.

The confusion of the priestly mind was lamentable. The aspirations expressed in short Gathic prayers were obscured by formulas detailing how many times to repeat them to ward off evil and terrorize demons. Their language was alleged to generate powerful vibrations when properly intoned, thus effectively transforming them into manthras (spells) capable of magically destroying works of evil and compelling the attention and responses of the divine powers.[6] For a growing list of items and activities, such as touching anything dead or that had been in contact with the dead, there was an understandably pre-scientific dread. But the degree to which preoccupation with things deemed loathsome was carried seems unrestrained, even as the confused mingling of mechanical error in cultic performance, physical contamination, and moral turpitude appears so irrational even for that time as still to be inexplicable. Perhaps the explanation for the survival of Zoroaster's more single-minded concern with moral issues as the ones of substantive consequences for human character is simply that good moral precepts can survive association with patent irrelevancies longer than one would think. In any event, they have.

Post-Avestan Times

The Sasanian renaissance for Zoroastrianism, after the centuries of Seleucid and Parthian rule when the religion languished, was almost by definition a restoration of the Later Avestan situation. After all, the present *Avesta* is only the little which the priests of the Sasanian era remembered of a body of Scripture already by then largely beyond recall. Since assumptions about the nature of lost material would be manifestly insupportable, the one hypothesis left is that the reconstituted material was remembered because it reflected best what had once obtained. In determining to make it the "constitution" for a restoration, the Sasanian kings and their high priests were re-affirming as authoritative the mixture of Zoroaster's Gathic ethic with ideas and rules derived from the Later Avestan penchant for considering all manner of essentially amoral cultic and cultural particularities as of the same order.

---

[6]Videvdat 19:8-10.

The Pahlavi literature of the post-Sasanian period provides further corroboration of this thesis.[7]   As Zaehner has shown by referring mainly to the *Denkard* of the ninth century,[8] the religion retained its three-fold emphasis on world and life affirmation, integrity as the ideal of character, and prudence in action.   The goals of earthly life were health for both body and soul, happiness in prosperity, and the clear conscience that is the reward for charity to one's neighbour. If the higher goal of life in a heaven seemed to make the good earthly life only a physical means to a spiritual end, it was to be remembered—as the doctrine of this period explained— that the final resolution would unite bodies and souls parted by death even as it would reunite the alienated world with paradise.

Once one knows the virtues to be prized, the vices to be avoided may be readily inferred: asceticism or its opposite—lust, pride, dishonesty, greed, sloth, and selfishness.

The problems for the religion of the good life, however, were that higher premiums were placed upon restoring the neglected cultus and indulging in theological speculation than on teaching the principles by which to live one's daily life. Under the Sasanians, the rehabilitated priesthood had the reconstituted *Avesta* to memorize and the rubrics of the cultus to restore. That the attention given to these tasks was far from grudging is verified by the *Rivayats*, the series of answers which priests in Persia addressed to many sets of questions asked of them by Parsis over a period of about three

---

[7]It is believed that the earliest exegetical commentaries, in Pahlavi, date from immediately after the reconstitution of the canon (i.e., the attenuated *Avesta*), but that the Muslim conquerors of the seventh century systematically destroyed them in their zeal to establish their own religion. In any case, the surviving tracts date mainly from the ninth through the eleventh centuries, after the more tolerant Abbasid Caliphs had succeeded the zealous Umayyads as the authorities of Islam in the Persian world. (See Dhalla, *History*, pp. 320-321.) The exceptions would be earlier morality tracts belonging to a genre known as *Handarz* (admonitions). Much of their value lies in revealing that Zoroaster's basic elementary principles had at least not been forgotten and could, on occasion, be affirmed without an admixture of cultic counsel. They do not appear, however, to represent increasingly critical and profound ways of applying elementary principles to the problems of life and society. (See, for example, *Citak Handarz I. Poryotkesan;* translated and edited by Maneck F. Kanga, Bombay, 1960).

[8]The summary which follows paraphrases Zaehner, *Dawn and Twilight*, pp. 276 ff.

centuries (Dhalla gives 1478 and 1766 as their outside dates). Some matters of morals and justice were treated, but most of the issues were cultic and, sometimes, theological. When cultic, the issue might be the proper performance of a liturgical rite. Perhaps more often than not, it was a matter of how to perform with cultic propriety some action which should have been categorized simply as social custom and governed by common sense. Thus for example, the judgment was rendered that a menstruous woman should approach no closer than thirty steps from a person "performing the kusti." Even the matter of the proper posture for a man urinating, and the question of how far the stream may be directed in front of his feet without his sinning cultically were dignified by requiring a priest's formal opinion.[9]

The theological imagination of the time found expression in new tracts fancifully embroidering with details the more economical notions of early Zoroastrianism. The cosmogony of the Gathas and Avestan references to legendary history running back to the time of creation are hardly more than suggestive outlines of the unknown past. The Pahlavi tracts, however, supplied the minutiae that satisfied believers' naive curiosity about realms and times more exciting than their own. Images of the future, and of heavens and hells beyond the bounds of mundane terrestrial space, also were unveiled, their supply keeping pace with demand.[10]

In short, the times did not provide a favorable climate for adventures in moral theology and profound ethical reflection. An earlier post-Sasanian period of Muslim intolerance and repression had passed, but the struggle for survival sapped creative energies. It was easier to dream than to struggle, to be a spectator cheering for the victory of divine forces over demonic power than to become a soldier fighting for the victory of righteousness. "The Zoroastrian

---

[9]Ervad Bamanji Nusserwanji Dhabhar, *The Persian Rivayats of Hormazyar Framarz and Others* (Bombay: The K.R. Cama Oriental Institute, 1932), p. 32 and p. 101. See also Dhalla, *History,* p. 458, for other examples.

[10]Many orthodox and conservative Zoroastrians are loath to admit that the Pahlavi doctrinal tracts were "contemporary fiction," preferring to believe instead that their content was essentially Avestan—i.e., based upon lost portions of the Later Avesta. This seems improbable. If their content was known, then there is need to explain why the Avestan texts themselves could not be recalled and included (or were recalled but not included) in the reconstituted Sasanian canon.

community of Persia, during these centuries," in Dhalla's judgment, "lay steeped in the grossest ignorance and darkness .... It was manifest that the pristine purity of the faith had departed with the greatness and glory of the Iranian nation!"[11]

The Religion of the Good Life in the Twentieth Century

Cut off from their ancestral compatriots by migration to India, the Parsis preserved their traditional manners and morals partly because these provided their self-identity as a community and strengthened the impulses to be mutually supportive that were necessary to survival; partly also because a certain amount of cultural separatism was helpful in reassuring native Indians that they had come neither to conquer by force nor to dominate by influence. At the same time, according to their lore, they may well have been at pains to stress similarities between customs and by adaptation maintain a low profile. In any event, they were afforded toleration, and while they preserved their ethnic distinctiveness, their integrity and enterprise won them, over the centuries, a respected niche in Indian society. It was this kind of successful adjustment that stood them in good stead when the British presence, as the East India Company, reached the west coast in the late seventeenth century and took over, as the government itself, at the beginning of the nineteenth.

The principal occupations taken up by the various contingents of Parsis arriving from Iran had been those of farming, weaving, carpentry, miscellaneous trading, and the brewing of today. But alone among India's ethnic groups, they had no caste system. Freed of the hampering burden of caste tabus, they could make themselves useful to Europeans doing business or having colonial stakes in India. They were thus prepared to do the same for the British, serving them first in coastal centers where the Parsis themselves were concentrated and then gravitating with their mentors in large numbers to the developing city of Bombay.

The Parsis' traditional virtues were precisely those which led to their employment—honesty, industry, prudence, and trustworthiness —even as these had always been conducive—on Indian soil—to their health and modest prosperity. Even so, they might have remained aides had it not been for their perception that education conjoined with fluency in English could fit them to become their

---

[11]Dhalla, *History*, pp. 444-445.

employers' peers. Accepting every opportunity, they were soon trusted with responsibilities offering them positions in which they could exercise power and earn their own shares of profit alongside the British, and it was only one step from there to their own entrepreneurship. They took that step and thus, during the nineteenth century, the history of west coast India became one that could not be written without chronicling the Parsis' phenomenal enterprise in the fields of business, manufacturing, building and construction, education, medicine, law, government and social welfare.

Personal Morality

The integrity which was the heart beat of the Parsis' achievements had almost nothing for its "life-blood" except the time-honored moral admonition to live by "good thoughts, good words, good deeds" (*Humata, Hu'chta, Huvarshta*). No systematic education for the moral nurture of the laity has ever been attempted except by a miniscule number of priests. A few publications, most of them privately printed, now and then cite the traditional ideals and virtues of Zoroastrians, but, given the lack of institutional mechanisms for fostering widespread distribution of such materials, they have few readers. The priests could be influential in a pastoral sense if they were better educated, but since they are not, the great majority of them do not help the laity to distinguish between cultic rectitude and moral uprightness, or conversely, between cultic impropriety and moral turpitude.

This may be illustrated by referring to how the Parsis have treated matters of individual conduct or "private" morality. Smoking, for example, is tabu for most Parsis because they say the smoke, mixed with the poisonous carbon dioxide of exhaled breath, pollutes fire. However, recent generations whose education has included study of the empirical sciences have more and more questioned why they should feel *moral* guilt for breaking a cultic tabu, itself archaic, when for them smoking seems an amoral matter of personal choice commonly allowed by social custom.[12]

---

[12] It is ironic that the tendency to impute moral taint for breaking with this cultic tabu was meeting with the greatest skepticism and smoking was on the increase just when really moral issues were surfacing in the form of questions about the effects of smoking on health, smokers' lack of consideration for the sensitivities of non-smokers, and the ethics of spending for tobacco treasure which could bring relief to some of the hungry poor. But so far these issues

The same trend is more apparent in the West where the great majority of the Zoroastrian urbanites are of Indian Parsi background rather than Iranian. Once rites or periodic "congregational" meetings are concluded, there is no constraint upon smoking while socializing. In Iran, however, there is neither tabu to honor nor trend to mention. Some informants vaguely remember hearing about the tabu, but association with a cross-section of the Zoroastrians of several communities provides ample opportunity to observe smoking by priests and lay members of governing anjumans as well as by laity who are Zoroastrian merely by birth and habit.

The strictures to which the orthodox Parsis subject those who are casual or careless in their observance of the various padyabs of the day, or who wear the sudreh and kusti only on ceremonial occasions, also clearly suggest moral indignation about cultic impropriety. But again, the trend, especially outside of India, is visibly toward pruning away the moral connotations traditionally associated with cultic conventions. Iranian informants articulate the distinction clearly when they say that donning the sudreh and kusti at Navjote merely denotes conscious affirmation of one's identity and that afterward it is not what is worn but what a person aspires to *be* and strives to *do* with his life that is of any real consequence.[13]

One of the Zoroastrians' characteristic moral traits has always been sobriety. Undoubtedly, the ever-emphasized good thoughts flowing from Good Mind and the virtue of prudence in action have had their effects. In any case, intoxication is looked upon as subversive to clear thinking and right aspiration, and as indicative of flabby moral character. On the other hand, neither legal prohibition nor abstinence by personal choice has ever been regarded as a moral imperative. Drinking in moderation is enjoyed and the means for doing so are usually made available when people entertain at home or gather communally for the ceremonies with which feasting is associated. Whether in modern times the greater freedom for youth from traditional family influences on behavior will result in a higher incidence of marked intemperance is not yet known.

---

have not received the attention that would encourage abstinence as effectively as did the cultic tabu.

[13]The reference is mainly to inner garments. The styles of the other garments of Zoroastrians have always blended with those of the region of residence. The principal exceptions have been the dress for priests and the curious but now virually abandoned hats for men.

Much will depend upon whether succeeding generations, in shaping their response to the community's particular problems, manage to preserve the religion as a vital centering force in life.

Sexual Ethics

The sexual ethic of Zoroastrians has been shaped in great measure by their consistent disapproval of asceticism and the threats to their survival posed by historical exigencies. The *Avesta* makes marriage a sacred duty and parenthood the ideal state. Priests have the additional reason for marrying that their vocation became hereditary. The nobility of Achaemenid times enjoyed the deviations represented by harems and eunuchs; but monogamy, the essential equality of the sexes, and conjugal love and fidelity were in practice the norms for most commoners. That is not to say there were no plural marriages. Both polygamy and concubinage were allowed from earliest times until well into this century if a man needed to go that far to have a healthy and surviving son.[14]

The Parsis' migration to India resulted in exposure to the dominant Hindu customs and, as time passed, in making considerable accommodation to them. Many of the details of the Parsis' early social history are not chronicled, but it is known that by the seventeenth century "polygamy by males was . . . [still] prevalent" and "child marriage quite common." Some sets of parents even made provisional oral contracts to wed their as yet unborn children.[15]

The *practice* of bigamy very nearly ceased in the early nineteenth century when just provisions were made for divorce. Ending child marriage proved more difficult. Bulsara has noted that Iranian Zoroastrians advised the Parsis in 1670 that 14 and 10 were the appropriate minimal ages for boys and girls, respectively, to marry. The Parsis, however, were unresponsive until reformist sentiment in their own community, developing little by little over a period of two centuries, finally effected voluntary compliance with the Iranian

[14]See Miles Menander Dawson, *The Ethical Religion of Zoroaster* (New York: AMS Press, 1969), reprinted from the edition of 1931, p. 148. The justification for plural marriage by modern Parsis, according to Dawson (in 1931) was still that of a man's needing a son to survive him, but he implies that monogamy was otherwise mandatory (p. 149).

[15]Jal F. Bulsara, "Social Reform among the Parsis," the Evelyn Hersey Memorial Lectures – 1968 (Delhi: University of Delhi, School of Social Work, 1938), p. 17.

norm and eventually the passage in 1929 of an act which introduced penalties for marriages of girls under 14 and of boys under 18.[16] Fifty years later, urban Parsis among whom the average marrying age is well up in the twenties must sometimes long for the "good old days," since their greater concern has come to be the number who are marrying non-Parsis or not marrying at all.

With monogamy established as the one form of marriage, the traditional ideal of the institution as a relationship defined by mutual respect, responsibility, and fruitfulness has prevailed with Zoroastrians everywhere. There are other problems, however, which today are becoming matters of conscience. A long standing penchant for the marriage of cousins—said to have its origin in Magian preference for it—is being questioned on the ground that it is genetically inadvisable, and if not healthy, then morally suspect. The reason for worrying about late marriage, among the Parsis, is that it results in having fewer children than would otherwise be the case, or even in having none at all. Yet remaining single is worse. Both phenomena are known to be on the increase,[17] as is also marriage outside the community. The latter is not a major issue in Iran where Zoroastrians are willing to accept spouses who are converts, but for the Parsis all three options are viewed as in some measure failure to honor moral imperatives mandated by Zoroaster himself.

Until the late nineteenth century, Zoroastrian sexual morality was essentially the morality of marriage and parenthood. This made adultery the sexual vice most likely to come to mind as the substance of sexual immorality. Prostitution and "unnatural crime" were other recognized vices,[18] but it was hardly supposed that Zoroastrians ever practiced them. When Karaka asserted in 1884

[16]*Ibid.*, pp. 24-25.

[17]See Sapur Faredun Desai, *A Community at the Cross-Road, op. cit.*, pp. 43-44.

[18]Sheriarji Dadabhai Bharucha, *A Brief Sketch of the Zoroastrian Religion and Customs* (Bombay: D.B. Taraporevala Sons & Co., 1928), p. 58. This small work by Bharucha, an Ervad, appears to be unusual in that it contains a detailed list of sins and vices to be avoided by Zoroastrians, whereas most Parsis whose works are of similar thematic genre normally cite only the virtues for which noble forebears have been justly famous. There is no hint from Bharucha, however, that the prostitution and unnatural vice—which other writers never seem to think to mention though they may, like Bharucha, cite the tradition's consistent stand against adultery—had any practitioners.

that Bombay had not even one Parsi prostitute,[19] such was his authority as an historian that the statement quickly passed into the public domain to be used without quotation marks by anyone interested in recounting again the Zoroastrians' heroic victories over every threat to their lives and honor.

Today, the new communities formed by migration are small and self-conscious, the members knowing one another well enough to minimize anonymity. They are middle class, industrious, and respectable. Though they too have the problem of late marriage, there is no evidence suggesting that the problem has as yet led to compromise with the "puritan" sexual ethic of their tradition. Similar standards prevail in Iran where the fragility of religious freedom, never wholly out of mind, prompts the Zoroastrians as a small minority to preserve all the substance of unassailable moral rectitude.

The situation among urban Parsis in India is less exactly discerned, but rumors abound that would grieve Karaka. The liberal milieu of cosmopolitan cities, the opportunity afforded for anonymity, and the increasing incidence of poverty among Bombay's Parsis in recent decades[20] are factors which lend credence at least to the allegations of non-Parsi men that Parsi prostitutes are quite available. Equally common is talk about the emergence of homosexuality and its increase among young males as a consequence of the trend toward marrying late. The fact that parental initiative has little place today in shaping the socio-sexual patterns and decisions of marriageable youth may be another causative factor producing change. Men who are unattracted by those of the women whom they find plain and yet are heedful of the community's continuing objection to intermarriage may—it can be imagined—accommodate themselves to bachelorhood after finding the supply of attractive women unequal to demand, but to bachelorhood with sex rather than without it. An astute social scientist with investigative skill

---

[19]Karaka, *History of the Parsis*, I, *op. cit.*, p. 99. How accurately informed Karaka was cannot be known. If there were any Parsi prostitutes in his day, they would almost certainly have concealed either their occupation or their identity as Parsis.

[20]At mid-century, the number of Parsis in Bombay receiving from communal funds some form of direct aid becasuse of poverty amounted, according to informed estimate, to 20% of the city's 60,000 Parsis. See P.A. Wadia, *Parsis Ere the Shadows Thicken*, *op. cit.*, p. 14.

might secure some empirical data that would supplant present rumors with information, but at present discreet efforts to gain introduction by Parsis to social workers, physicians, or others who might be conduits of information about either prostitution or homo-sexuality meet only with polite confessions of ignorance. Such "im-moralities" are either not attractive to enough Parsis for their practice to become known and a matter of concern or they are regarded as deviations too painful or embarrassing to discuss.

The Socio-economic Ethic

When Zoroastrians confront broader issues of social policy, the premise of their ethic is that charity and philanthropy are enjoined for ameliorating personal and societal ills. One should have concern for the welfare of his neighbor, and the person that the Zoroas-trian is most likely to think of first as fitting the definition of "neighbor" is another Zoroastrian. Zoroaster's position was that the purest and noblest brotherly love should be shown to other worshipers of Ahura Mazda, but those who stubbornly and repeatedly refused to turn from daeva worship deserved the treat-ment of enemies.

No very deep or systematic reflection was given to the social ethic during the centuries of post-Achaemenid foreign rule. Not even during the Sasanian restoration did ethics come in for serious examination. When the priests were not attempting the fragmentary re-constitution of the *Avesta* and re-learning neglected rites, they were fighting off the influence of foreign religions, the rise of new ones, and the dissemination of allegedly heretical versions of their own religion. Meanwhile, the masses were reduced to poverty and misery either to pay for kings' wars or to enrich the two privileged classes, the priesthood and the landed aristocracy. Taraporewala's brief but sharply etched sketch of the period in an essay on Mazdak-ism notes the tragic consequences of "fratricidal strife between the Christians and the Zoroastrians," of the masses "being ground down relentlessly by the vested interests," and of the desperation which made Mazdak's followers oblivious to the fact that his radically communistic social policy was, as remedy, no less evil than the conditions which prompted it.[21]

---

[21]Taraporewala, *The Religion of Zarathushtra, op. cit.*, pp. 170-172. The popularity of the revolutionary Mazdak's late fifth century movement was such

Under Muslim rule, Zoroastrians became a depressed minority. Even in India, where waves of Iranian emigres and a favorable birth rate were to make the Zoroastrians more numerous than in Iran, they were still a minority, not depressed perhaps, but struggling. It is not inappropriate, therefore, to characterize Zoroastrians as having an outlook which for most of their history—with the possible exception of the late Achaemenid period—was shaped by a "seige mentality." Under such circumstances, energies are consumed in struggling merely to survive, and there are none left over for investment in the task of re-shaping the world! This makes understandable the Zoroastrian disposition to shape only their own corner of the world by prospering economically, with those who succeed in accepting responsiblity for removing or diminishing the disabilities of those who fail.

The practical consequences with greatest visibility are the many institutions which Parsi philanthropists have built and funded. There are schools, colleges, and institutes for students at all educational levels, hospitals both general and specialized, housing colonies for co-religionists who might otherwise not find decent homes available (or if available, affordable), the compounds for festival rites and ceremonies, and--not to be forgotten—the grounds, bunglis, and dakhmas for the dead and the obsequies conducted by those who mourn their passing.

The philanthropy made visible only by records and reports of benefits bestowed has taken the form of a great number of trust funds established for many reasons, some related to objective and perennial needs, others reflecting the subjective or curious notions of donors with pet causes to promote. Endowments for use in meeting the realistically conceived needs have provided scholarships, paid students' school fees, underwritten medical treatment, distributed regular food allotments or stipends for its purchase by needy persons, and supported a number of projects of benefit to priests and their families, most of whom are to be counted among the community's poor. The list is not exhaustive; the whole one represents a great investment in meeting the minimal needs of a large number of persons in want or trouble. Too many endowments, however, were

---

that his teachings survived *sub rosa* for several centuries after his murder by treachery. He preached a radical egalitarianism and is reputed to have urged common ownership of all possessions including wives.

founded out of motives colored by sentimentality, or eccentricity, or illusions of their eternal relevance. The legal impediments to redefining the purposes to which income from these endowments may be devoted are formidable and in some instances decisive, particularly when joined with the resistance of trustees sharing the original founders' lack of perspicacity.

The conclusion to which analysis points is that the social ethic, by continuing to extol the virtues of individual ambition and industry, kindness to neighbor, charity for the needy, and generosity in endowments for the enjoyment of the community, is admittedly an ethic, but one that is limited socially by its ethnic parochialism. While many of the endowed institutions have offered some facilities or services to a limited number of non-Zoroastrians or are—as in the case of most hospitals and scientific institutes—unrestricted altogether, the wider community has found itself served mainly indirectly, in the sense that everyone benefits to some extent by the business acumen of those who create a thriving economy, employment opportunities, a climate of honesty in management of affairs, and a market for the services of professionals such as lawyers and physicians. General benefits are thus less the effects of conscious ethical concern than of the smooth functioning of the economy, in which case the question arises as to how charitable people will be if or when bad times follow.

The problem at base is really that there are no trained ethicists— just as there are virtually no professional theologians or critical philosophers—among Zoroastrians. There can therefore be no critical theorizing, no lively debate between theorists and no ever-more-carefully-and-relevantly-conceived ethic for them to ponder and with conscious conscientiousness apply. And this lack results in doing things out of unexamined motives and simplistic ineffective ways. Professor Wadia, after perusing the wording of documents describing and governing endowments that were supporting charities in Bombay in the 1940s concluded tersely that "the motive behind their creation was more to open the prospects of heaven to the donors than to minister to the uplift of the afflicted."[22]

The management and administration of charities also, Wadia found, leaves much to be desired. Most of the funds have operated with staffs of good intentioned but untrained persons. Inefficiency

---

[22] Wadia, *op. cit.*, p. 15.

and waste seem endemic. Even more serious, perhaps, is the persistence of an outlook on the part of such non-professionals which Wadia deemed "medieval." "We still continue to talk in terms of doles," he reported, "instead of . . . benefits,"[23] of giving a small amount of relief rather than helping to change the conditions which are disabling.

A balanced view requires respect for the immensity of the outlays made for charitable purposes by the uniformly-altruistic rich families. The foundations (numbering about 1,000) over which the Bombay Paris Panchayat has exercised some supervision, may be credited, on the one hand, with the fact that Parsis have never— until recently, at least—been reduced to public beggary and, on the other, with having achieved by their investment in education the highest literacy rate of any religio-ethnic group in India.[24]

In Iran and the West, as in India, the moral standards of Zoroastrians are largely those of the educated classes of the non-Zoroastrian majorities with whom they have association in daily life. One thing to be noted about the Iranian Zoroastrians, however, is that their traditional emphasis on integrity and moral rectitude is viewed as somewhat distinctive in that country. It had gone unnoticed, of course, as long as Zoroastrians remained a submerged minority. But in this century, when they have been relatively free to rise economically and socially to levels consonant with their abilities, many have migrated from the isolated rural communities to the cities where their reputation for trustworthiness has opened opportunities for them in banking, commerce and industry, major professions, and government service. Those who, like their Parsi cousins before them, have succeeded as entrepreneurs in amassing wealth, have then proceded to be guided by the same social ethic, namely that of expressing brother love by philanthropy. The beneficiaries most usually cited in Zoroastrian news media are disadvantaged communities, such as those of rural Iran which lack means to afford priests recruited from India. Then there are the newer Western communities which, though their members may prosper, are not yet large enough collectively to afford institutional accommodation for social and religious functions.[25] Only in Greater London, where the community

[23]*Ibid.*, p. 22.
[24]See Eckhard Kulke, *The Parsees, op. cit.*, pp. xviii and xix.
[25]In Iran, for example, the priest brought from India to serve the fire-temple

is older, have facilities been acquired without undue reliance on philanthropic aid. But this is as much as the English Zoroastrians have managed. They have prospered and enjoyed a good middle class existence but in an era which postdates the Industrial Revolution and its opportunities for family fortune-building.

The Socio-political Ethic

Whether the social ethic, then, is expressed in economic terms by the great benefactions of the wealthy or by small donations to Zoroastrian causes, a significant component of the motivation for service is the sense of responsibility for the material welfare of one's own ethnic-religious community. There seems to be no common concern, however, much less any argued justification, for construing *political* activity as a second way of giving expression to the social ethic. It may be that the centuries-long exclusion of Zoroastrians from the political process after the Muslim conquest habituated them to political passivism. Certainly, in any case, this was the stance which the Parsi immigrants in India found appropriate, given their status as uninvited refugees wholly dependent upon the ruling Indians' hospitality for their survival.

Not until creeping English rule had finally replaced that of earlier masters did Parsis become known for some connection with the political order. Even then, for some it was a connection established by appointment rather than choice and the consequence, moreover, of economic rather than political service to the commonweal. Thus Cowasji Jehanghier Readymoney and a nephew, Cowasji Jehanghir, whom he adopted as a son, were knighted, in 1872 and 1895 respectively, for their public charities. The son was later made a Baronet as well, becoming one of the three Parsis whom the English crown so honored in the course of creating, overall, only five Indian Baronets while ruling the country.[26]

This is not to say there were not some few Parsis who at the same

in Yazd is paid by Teheran philanthropists dealing in industrial machinery. The venerable Teheran philanthropist generally thought to be the wealthiest of Iran's Zoroastrians, with a fortune based on textiles, has made donations enabling the Zoroastrians of Greater New York, Chicago, and Toronto to establish centers for social gatherings, religious education, and such ritual observances as may be held outside a dedicated fire-temple.

[26]See P.P. Bulsara, *Highlights of Parsi History* (Bombay: P.P. Bulsara, 1963), n. 70, p. 52.

time were taking to politics as a matter of conscience. Among those who did was Dadabhai Naoroji, three times President of the Indian National Congress (in 1886, 1893, and 1906), author of *Povery and Un-British Rule in India*, and the first of the three Indians—all Parsis - ever to occupy seats by election to the British Parliament between 1892 and 1929.[27]

The high visibility of a few very gifted leaders nevertheless should not be taken as evidence that a majority of the Parsis have ever foresaken political passivism for activism. As Kulke has perceived, their identification with the British and the prosperity resulting from their association set them apart from most Indians whose increasingly passionate desire was for independence.[28] Nor is this contradicted by the fact that Parsis at the turn of the century, though a minority in Bombay, occupied a larger number of the elected seats in the Municipal Council than any of the city's four other ethnic groups. The Britsh still controlled a sizable number of the seats filled by other means than election. The affinity felt by the Parsis with the incumbents of these seats, together with the fact that the concerns of a Council were those of local politics, may be taken to mean only that Parsis were doing their civic duty rather than finally experimenting with serious political application of their social ethic. This impression is supported by the Parsis' acceptance of a subordinate role even in local politics when expansion of the franchise increased the opportunities of other groups to wield more political power.[29]

National independence, granted in 1947, gave the great Hindu majority its first opportunity in centuries to exchange the role of servant for that of master and thus at last to dominate the political arena. The effect upon the Parsis was reinforcement of their minority status and their essentially apolitical consciousness. Not that they have been indifferent to government. Their competence in business and the professions has continued to bring them appointments to high posts in the judiciary, the armed services, advisory and regulatory agencies, and the like. There are scattered instances also of their election to political office at both local

---

[27]*Ibid.*, p. 68. Other Parsis held the Congress Presidency twice in its early history and one was its General Secretary for several years before and after the turn of the century.

[28]See Kulke, *op. cit.*, p. xx.

[29]Again, see Kulke, p. xxi.

and national levels. But the abilities to which such appointments or elections bear witness are not especially valued by Parsis for the contribution they could make to forging a Zoroastrian socio-political ethic. Parsis of note are more useful to other Parsis as justifiers of an "elite consciousness" the preservation of which helps them to "forget the actual dangers to the community's future."[30] Even the office-holders themselves take no lead in defining a theory of political duty grounded in religious conviction. There is no *Zoroastrian* theory of the just war for example, or of the rights of the state *vs* the rights of its citizens, or even of the nature of the relationship that should obtain between the state and the country's institutions of religion.

In Iran, political impotence was a price long willingly paid for whatever peace and security the ruling Muslims would allow a religious minority if it kept a low profile. The situation changed somewhat during the recent Pahlavi period when the constitution of the country provided for token minority representation in the parliament. A few Zoroastrians also received appointments to positions in the bureaucracy where competence and trustworthiness without need of surveillance were needful qualifications. At the same time, their slowly improving situation provided occasion for a strain on conscience. Though pleased with recognition of their existence and capabilities, they were painfully aware that it was received from a regime increasingly corrupt and oppressive. The Iranian restoration of theocracy signals retirement to political obscurity again for Zoroastrians - and limbo for any new political ethic that might have been in the making there.

If there is any evidence that the Western Zoroastrians may supply the missing political dimension of their ethic, it has not been publicized. Their house organs and news dispatches to parent communities emphasize as their concerns (1) the courage and hard work necessary to finding good employment and subsequent security in lands newly adopted, (2) the need to surmount the difficulties of preserving the religion despite the lack of familiar institutional supports, and (3) the *pros* and *cons* of departures from tradition which are simply unavoidable or which changed settings are perceived as having made optional and subject to fresh appraisal. These are

---

[30]Kulke, *The Parsees in India* (Delhi: Vikas Publishing House, Pvt. Ltd., 1974), p. 268.

concerns having no bearing at all on politics though some connection may be discerned between them and what morality enjoins by way of obligation to one's community of faith.[31]

The typical Zoroastrian then is a person who honors rectitude, charity, diligence, and stewardship. His pattern is the character that tradition has ascribed to the Prophet; and the lessons he has learned about how life should be lived, he has found in the Gathas.

Yet his situation is curiously anomalous, in that his ideal of personal integrity is neither derived from nor supported by a more comprehensive social ethic. Nor is it significantly inspired or reinforced by the rituals of the cultus.[32] He is possessed still of impressive moral status, but the corporate community has no tradition of providing the seriously argued and carefully articulated social principles needful for guiding action when the dilemmas are societal and require a united strategy—and not merely the goodwill of each honest *Zarthosti*.

---

[31]It can now be understood why Kulke would conclude that historically as well as contemporaneously the essential substance of the Zoroastrians' political ethic has been strict loyalty to the ruling authority in the interest of survival. *Ibid.*, pp. 133-134f.

[3] It is probably true to say that the cultus, in its relation to morality, is a source of more confusion than support. Its tendency to encourage the erasure of all distinction between moral purity and cultic purity inclines the Zoroastrian to view cultic correctness with approbation of the same genre that might more properly be reserved for purity of heart and good personal hygiene. This observation should not be regarded, however, as applicable to Zoroastrians everywhere. Urban Iranian and Western Zoroastrians find that many traditional cultic rites and their meanings are archaic and, in any case, not practieable in new cultural settings.

CHAPTER 6

Persisting Concerns

Three times Zoroastrian Persia fell to conquerors seeking mainly political power and economic enrichment. Each time, Zoroastrianism was weakend in one way or another. The last time, of course, was the worst, since the Arabs used their Muslim religion to justify conquest and sooner or later imposed it upon the vanquished, by zealous persuasion if possible, otherwise by threats and force.

The fear of total extinction for the religion of Zoroaster was ultimately eased only by the flight of the stubbornly faithful to India. There they enjoyed toleration and equal status with native ethnic groups. Freedom, conjoined with sturdy character and ambition, provided the climate conducive to achievement. Thus, in due time, the prospering community shook off the seige mentality that oppression had fostered and began to glory in its capacity to survive hardship and rise again.

Parsi literature of the late nineteenth and early twentieth centuries was imbued with the sense of pride in accomplishment. Even in Iran, where the policy of imposing civil disabilities on the surviving Zoroastrians had finally been dropped, attitudes of confidence and optimism were reappearing. Yet not for long, at least as regards the Parsis. By the 1950s, warnings of decline were being sounded. More and more, the printed word was marked by foreboding, engendering fears that could apparently be held in tolerable check only by repeated recitations of the saga of surviving in times past by dint of heroic opposition to seemingly overwhelming odds. The theme became, in fact, so common that among Parsis not allergic to change on principle, there finally arose a suspicion that the stories of ancestral heroism were serving no longer as spurs to action but as substitutes for it. The issue, posed succinctly by a Pakistani Parsi in the 1970s was one of having

. . . so blinded ourselves with our self-woven cocoon of past glory,

that we are unable to make a rational judgement on our own dege-
neration. . . because we. . . survived Alexander and the Arabs, we
[think we] shall survive into the distant future by the Grace of
Ahura Mazda, even if we sit with folded arms, and do nothing. . .[1]

The crisis is multifaceted, with virtually no aspect of it standing in
unrelated isolation from the others.

The Sheer Survival Problem

The gravest of all issues for the Zoroastrians is that of their
numerical shrinkage. Aside from the several thousands of Iranians
and the small communities such as the one in England, the 114, 890
Parsis in India (and, after partition, West Pakistan) *were* the Zoroastrians of the world and were still on the increase as late as 1941.
Twenty years later, their number had diminished by nearly 14%,
and after another ten years, by 9%, leaving a total of 91,266.[2]
There was little comfort to be gained by hoping that the migration
drain in the direction of Iran and the West would explain everything.
The communities there did not report increases comparable to the
loss. Moreover, local statistics were supplying other reasons. In
Greater Bombay, where nearly two-thirds of the Parsis live, deaths
exceeded births by 101 in 1961. By 1970, the difference had increased to 385, with deaths on the increase and births decreasing. The
principal causes of death over the last half of the decade were acci-
dents, cancer, cardiac failure, haemorrhage, influenza-pneumonia,
old age, senile debility, and uraemia.[3] The list echoed, in part, one
made by Desai nearly a quarter-century earlier, but Desai's focus
had been on types of life-shortening illnesses tending to be hereditary or traceable to syndromes of living conditions in bad housing.
Thus tuberculosis, respiratory diseases, diabetes, mental illness, and
retardation were special foci for his concern. They might not be the
immediate cause of death, but their effect was to shorten life and
add to the death toll.

[1] Homi B. Minocher Homji, *O Whither Parsis? Placate and Perish or Reform
and Flourish?* A study of Community Introspection (Karachi, 1978), p. x.

[2] Ratan Rustomji Marshall, ''Parsi Population Problem,'' *Rahe Asha* (The
Path of Righteousness), published by the Federation of the Parsi Zoroastrian
Anjumans of India, June 1977, p. 28.

[3] Trustees of the Parsi Punchayet Funds and Properties, Bombay, *Report for
the Year 1970*, pp. 21-23.

The Iranians alone, among Zoroastrians, were reporting actual though modest increase during the 1970s. Some converts were reported, though wisely not publicized. A climate of religious toleration also encouraged once-silent Zoroastrians to confess their religious allegiance to census takers. Other reasons cited for increase were that reasonably early marriage was still traditional and the significant percentage of Zoroastrians who were still rural made for a favorable birth rate.[4] However, a favorable national climate for this religious minority cannot be guaranteed, and the hope that the faith may be assured of renaissance by continuing increase in the land of its original birth would be less than firmly grounded.

Neither can the Western Zoroastrians be expected to counter the decline. They are almost exclusively urban and lacking in capital when migrating from India. They join the ranks mainly of the employed middle class and confirm the sociologists' observation that this class everywhere in the modern industrialized world voluntarily reduces its birth rate in the interest of security at least and upward mobility if possible.

Waning Fortunes

The economic health of the Parsis had been in decline well before it was noticed that the community was shrinking. In fact, many think that economic insecurity was an important factor in slowing the birth rate. Umrigar was but summarizing many a Parsi complaint when he wrote that the number of Parsi enterprises and industrial concerns, such as those that had produced great fortunes in a previous century, were "getting smaller year after year."[5] Instead of a spirit of entrepreneurship, he found acute unemployment afflicting the community, and a lack of vocational diversification pointing to the decline of ambition and pride in work. The community was producing clerks and white-collar workers, but not starting businesses or turning to craftsmanship or even petty selling ventures.

Obviously, there could not have been improvement since the early 1940s when Wadia found 23% of the employable Parsi males of Greater Bombay without work and more than half of them repre-

[4]Information from Ali A. Jafarey, of the Iranian Ministry of Culture and Arts, in Tehran, September 14, 1977.

[5]K.D. Umrigar, "Are the Parsis Dying Out? *The Illustrated Weekly of India,* August 29, 1971, p. 35. The author was President of the Maharashtra Union of Working Journalists.

sentative of economic classes already rated poor or destitute. He contended that the refusal to adjust to economic realities and a penchant for living beyond their means lay behind the Parsis' unwillingness to work at any honest labor. "Summing up," he wrote, ". . . poverty is not only an economic phenomenon but has become a general social phenomenon, affecting a substantial majority of families within the community."[6]

The housing situation has provided another index of erosion in the quality of life. The first housing colonies built with communal funds around the turn of the century were for Parsis with low income and, according to Wadia, were of such construction that they had in effect become slums.[7] New construction, however, has never kept up with the demand of single persons and families who, in increasing numbers, have been priced out of the private housing market. Consequently, over-crowding, over-burdened facilities, and deterioration for lack of proper maintenance have been endemic problems. The worst of the colonies, Wadia said searingly, had become for the children, especially boys, "a breeding ground of organised beggary and hooliganism."[8] Even some of the newer and better built ones, grateful as their tenants are to have them, tend to be graceless in design and miserly with amenities.

Personal and Family Life

No imagination is required to perceive that the quality of domestic and community life is severely affected by the spread of poverty and inferior housing. There are still some affluent Parsis who live well in their private homes or genteel apartments, but many more live austerely in tasteless quarters, making do with furnishings that were cheap when new and which, with age, are woefully drab. No wonder, then, that the youth, leery of marital responsibilities that could condemn them at the least to a lifetime of marginal existence,

[6]P.A. Wadia, *Parsis Ere the Shadows Thicken, op. cit.,* 1949, p. 9. Wadia's inquiries led him to conclude that at least 20% of Bombay's Parsis were receiving relief from communal funds in the form of doles, and he was not counting those receiving some kind of indirect aid (p. 14). Homji, seeking to explain the decline still continuing after forty years, concluded that "the rich of yester years became the upper-middle class traders of today; the upper-middle class became the middle-class fixed income earners; and the lower-middle class became the new poor of the community." *Op. cit.,* p. xii.

[7]See Wadia, p. 26,

[8]*Ibid.,* p. 33.

are postponing marriage to their late 20s or, by that time, deciding to enjoy the greater economic security they will have if they avoid it altogether.

The situation is in many ways a grim one. Among those who do marry, there is increasing incidence of resort to desertion and divorce as means of escape from the disabilities the marriage itself perpetrates.[9] Others hope to better themselves by marrying outside the community, much to the dismay of the traditionalists who believe in the genetic superiority of the Parsis as an ethnic group and therefore in endogamy, irrespective of the prospects for inter-marital felicity and improved fortune in given cases. Working with figures compiled in Bombay for the year 1970, it may be deduced that approximately 18% of the marriages were mixed.[10] This rate is in all probability higher than in Iran where the Zoroastrian drift to the cities and away from strict traditional mores began only in recent times. On the other hand, it is not as high as among Zoroastrians "overseas," where according to their principal chronicler, one-third of the marriages are exogamous.[11] This is a rate high enough to imply that marriage as an institution is not in trouble with Zoroastrians once they migrate from India. Whether marriage anywhere, however, and of whichever type, can be made fruitful enough to halt the population decline is another question.

Controversial Issues

So far, the problems described arise from situations the facts of which are not in dispute. They are bemoaned, but they are not denied. Proposed remedies, on the other hand, cannot be validated

[9]*Ibid.*, p. 35.

[10]*Report for the Year 1970, op. cit.,* p. 25. But see also Piloo Nanavutty, *The Parsis* (New Delhi:National Book Trust, India, 1977), p. 174, for the assertion that "intermarriages are becoming the norm rather than the exception." If this is the case, little heed has been paid to Desai's view that "socio-biologically this community is a wonder." Claiming endogamy as the reason for its surviving at all, he counseled Parsis "to keep out of inter-marriage" and the larger communities "to leave it strictly alone in the interests of the world at large and India herself in particular." *Op. cit.,* p. 165. The facts may be somewhere between the extremes of Nanavutty's generalization and Desai's separatist ideal.

[11]Jamshed Pavri, in interview, "Pardesi Parsis," with *Parsiana,* August-November 1977, p. 28. Pavri, honorary secretary of the Zoroastrian Association of British Columbia, published the first directory of Zoroastrians "overseas," in the 1960s.

unless tried; and there is hardly any conceivable remedy that doesn't founder on the rocks of someone's convictions before implementation can be attempted. In part, this is explained by the widely divergent opinions as to why problematic situations arose in the first place. Until Zoroastrians—mainly, the Parsi ones—can agree on causative reasons, they are unlikely to agree on solutions.

Endogamy versus Exogamy

The debate about types of marriage is a case in point. It is a fact that marriage within the community of faith was the tradition of centuries. It is fact that the tradition is crumbling. But what may be the facts for one Zoroastrian as to when and why the tradition came about will be dismissed as mere opinion by another.

It was Wadia's claim that the Parsis' ancestors in India "freely mingled by marriage . . . with the people of the land," and that they "managed to survive" because of it. He went on to ask rhetorically if they could hope now to survive by "a policy of rigid exclusivism and in-breeding, by becoming a caste" when the whole idea of caste was being discarded by all their neighbors.[12]

The principal reason for the defence of endogamy is that Zoroastrians regard identity, both ethnic and religious, as inherited from the father. The Parsis have therefore regarded the children of non-Zoroastrian fathers as ineligible for Navjote or inclusion in the community. That does not mean, however, that the marriage of a Zoroastrian male to a non-Zoroastrian is desirable, since it is a truism that children commonly receive their religious instruction from the mother in the home. Not only that, but her religious commitment is frequently stronger and her practice of religion more faithful than a father's. The result is that the inheritance of identity from the father notwithstanding, the children are likely to be drawn to the mother's faith. The meaning is clear: the Zoroastrian community stands to lose potential members whenever mixed marriage occurs.

The hope of halting the numerical decline has been behind the insistence of some traditionalists that the Parsis possess valued racial characteristics which depend upon heredity. As Dabu has categorically declared, the "preservation of their blood from getting mixed

---

[12]Wadia, *op. cit.*, p. 140.

with that of other races is a necessity."[13] The venerable Dastur Mirza explains that necesssity as having its ground in God's "own Laws" and adds that a "complex unity of purpose divine" makes it as impossible for a person to change his religion as to change his parents.[14]

This is the doctrine that Homji has characterized as "a mythical purism," declaring it "mainly responsible for decimating the very community it hopes to preserve."[15] Its utility is challenged also by an interviewer for *Parsiana* who, in introducing the remarks of several behdins about their attitudes toward mixed marriages, found the traditional restrictions having the effect of treating "people who can be an asset to the community" as "outcastes."[16] What those on both sides of the issue obviously recognize is that it cannot be discussed apart from their even more emotion-laden views about conversion.

Conversion

If the controversy provoked by raising the issue of conversions were a literal match that could set fires, the Parsis among Zoroastrians would have already become extinct in flaming holocausts. Their Iranian ancestors had suffered untold hardship unless they converted to Islam, and there has been no time since when the Zoroastrians of Iran could redress their grievance by *accepting* converts unless it could be done covertly. The exceptions are mainly of recent occurrence. Urbanization and mobility provide opportunities for becoming quietly dissociated from one community and joining another, and this the Iranis say is presently what is happening, with marriage to a Zoroastrian as the usual occasion for converting to the religion at the same time.

[13]Dabu, *Message of Zarathushtra, op. cit.*, p. 16.

[14]Dastur H.K. Mirza, "On Conversion and Converts in Zoroastrianism," *Parsiana*, August 1970, p. 33.

[15]Homji, *op. cit.*, p. xiii. Apparently the "mythical purism" Homji scourges had no dearth of defenders at the Third World Zoroastrian Congress of January 1978. Asphandiar D. Moddie, writing his "Impressions . . . " for *Parsiana* (March 1978), commented on the "euphoria" engendered by "impassioned pleas for the purity of the racial stock . . . " adding caustically, "Never did so little genetics go so far! For a moment one wondered whether one was at a Zoroastrian Congress or at a stud farm." (p. 31).

[16]Feroza Paymaster, "Would you Marry out of the Community?" *Parsiana*, December-January 1975, p. 30.

The Parsis in India have simply had a different experience. Popular lore has it that in gratitude for the right to settle, they agreed to maintain friendly association with their native benefactors and offer no threat to the peace by tampering with such basic social structures as the family and indigenous religion(s). The facts, however, will probably never be known. The early centuries of Parsi history in India are simply not chronicled.

Yet a tradition did develop to the effect that the Parsis had steadfastly protected their ethnic purity and the integrity of their religion by endogamy and an anti-conversion policy from the time of their first ancestors' arrival in India. Some partisans of separatism hark back even to pre-historic times and evolve an argument that depends upon giving their own definition to "conversion." If it means proselytism, they say, then Zoroaster never practiced it. All he did was urge his contemporaries to abandon the corruptions of an already ancient but by then decadent Mazdayasnism. According to Karkhanavala, "the mission of Zoroaster was to rid the Mazdayasni religion of the evil of devayasni and restore it to its pristine purity . . ." Zoroastrianism is thus merely a part of "the process of evolution within the Mazdayasni religion . . . ." The conclusion for him is clear. "Because Zoroaster did not convert, conversion of non-Mazdayasnan[s] is forbidden in the religion. That [moreover] is why marriage of a Mazdayasni with a non-Mazdayasni is tabood and is considered a grave sin . . ."[17]

---

[17]M.D. Karkhanavala, "Parsis, be true Mazdayasni-Zarathostis," *Memorial Volume*, Golden Jubilee, *op. cit.*, pp. 94-95. One of my informants credited K.R. Cama, for whom the Oriental Institute in Bombay is named, with having coined the term "pristine purity." It caught on and now everybody wants it! The orthodox who complain that the beliefs and practices enjoined by the *Avesta* and—they are equally sure—by Zoroaster himself are slowly being eroded by neglect, insist that their restoration in full would be recovery of Zoroastrianism's pristine purity. Reformers believe with equal conviction that Zoroaster's Gathic religion had a simplicity, profundity, and cogency which the Later Avesta nearly buried under a mass of trivia, superstition, and priestcraft. The pruning still has a good way to go, they think, before the pristine purity of Zoroaster's religion is recovered. It is also, of course, pristine purity which is claimed for all the varied positions that can be found lying somewhere between the two extremes of ultra-traditionalism and radical reformation!

Incidentally, the idea that Karkhanavala's version of ancient history should be judged on its own merits quite apart from his qualifications as an atomic research scientist has not been widely enough appreciated by the traditionalists who quote him to score points.

The matter is explained a little differently by Mirza. Though he too has assumed a long pre-Zoroastrian history for 'Mazdayasni Religion,' it is not to be regarded as possessing a pristine purity. The prophet "received and preached new revelations" essential to improving the religion already embraced by most Iranians. Mirza can then contend that acceptance of new revelation is not the same as adopting a new religion and so justify the broader generalization: "Never in the long and chequered history did Zoroastrians adopt a policy of conversion of Non-Zororstrians."[18]

One reason based upon practical considerations for refusing the admission of converts has appeared again and again in Parsi publications during the present century. As one of the younger Parsi scholars expresses it, an open-door policy would permit "a steady stream of people" to opt for the faith "not out of love, conviction or understanding, but merely to take advantage of . . . [Parsi] funds and charities."[19] The judgement rendered in the famous Parsi Panchayet Case[20] in 1908 has been highly effective in blocking this very outcome. Nevertheless, the issue doesn't die, nor has anyone been successful in clarifying for the orthodox community the difference between the purely religious privileges that converts could be granted and the social perquisites—such as access to subsidized housing, loan funds, dakhmas, etc.—to which by the wording of the donors' bequests they would have no right as non-Parsis.

Though the oldest of the Parsi strongholds may still be governed by traditional sentiment, there are voices being raised even there, and by members of newer anjumans in inland cities and abroad, who are ready to break rank and make a case for conversion, some basing it on scripture, some on history, others on either wisdom or necessity. Nanavutty, contending that an anti-conversion policy "is in direct contradiction to the teachings of Zarathustra," points out that

> . . . every Nyaesh and every Yasht in the *Khordeh Avesta*, the Book of Daily Prayers, ends with . . . 'May the knowledge, extent and fame of the commandments of the excellent religion of Mazda

[18]H.K. Mirza, "On Conversion," *Memorial Volume*, Golden Jubilee, *op. cit.*, p. 21.
[19]Homi B. Dhalla, "Proselytism, then what?" *Ibid* , p. 138.
[20]*Supra*, p. 69.

ever increase in the world, over all its seven regions. So may it be. I must attain this goal; I must attain this goal; I must attain this goal.'.1

Daruwalla, editorializing in the daily *Bombay Samachar*, has found his reason in history for refusing to believe that conversion is un-Zoroastrian. He cites a report, dated July 2, 1822, describing a Navjote ceremony for nine converts, with "many Parsis of well known families" present to celebrate the occasion. "Blessed is such activity," he quotes from the report's conclusion, for ". . . therein lies the security and the prestige of the community." Further evidence for use in his editorial was found in the newspaper, *Jam-e-Jamshed*. An article reporting the same event and claiming that "the number of such Juddins accepted in the Parsi community . . . runs into thousands," likewise drew the conclusion that many a convert had "added to the prestige of the Parsis."22

Arguments based on the wisdom or necessity of allowing conversion are usually related to the religious implications for the non-Zoroastrian spouse of mixed marriage and the children of such a marriage, not to the contingency of finding members of the general public clamoring for admission to the fold. The first explicit stand ever taken on the issue by an official body was embodied in a resolution voted by the delegates to a zonal conference of northern anjumans affiliated with the Federation of Parsi Zoroastrian Anjumans of India, meeting in New Delhi, January 22-23, 1977. Though "heatedly debated," sanction was eventually given to conversion by marriage and acceptance of the children of a mixed marriage, irrespective of which partner of the union is (or was) the non-Zoroastrian.23

Aside from Iran, the West provides most of the contemporary instances of departures from tradition by taking action with or without resolutions to prepare the way. The Association centered in Greater London is something of an exception, having been the first to organize in the Western Hemisphere and at a time when Parsis alone among Zoroastrians were migrating there. It seemed only natural to define membership as open to Parsi Zoroastrians. They

---

21Nanavutty, *op. cit.*, pp. 174-175.
22Jehan Daruwalla, "Truth changes with time,"editorial in *Bombay Samachar*, August 28, 1977, p. 15.
23*Parsiana*, June-July 1977, p. 23.

also made "Special Resolutions" constitutionally dependent upon approval by three-fourths of those attending a Special General Meeting (the kind of meeting at which policy issues may be raised). The result is that a "vociferous minority" can defeat any proposal lacking overwhelming support.[24] One further factor explaining the Association's conservatism, which bends only far enough to allow "participation in all activities," is the number of members who are of the Athornan class and, although engaged in other occupations, have sufficient priestly training to render avocational service as performers of outer ceremonies. It is not a class which, when compared with the behdins—among the Parsis at least—is providing its proportionate share of reformers.

This leaves most of the improvisational action to the more numerous but individually smaller communities of North America and the South Pacific where response to exigency is the price of survival. Pavri, of Vancouver, has been substituting the term "community members" for "Parsis" or "*Zarthostis*" as a result of finding, first, that "overseas, every third marriage is a mixed marriage," and second, that "the non-Parsis of non-*Zarthosti* spouses take greater interest . . . than community members who are supposed to be *Zarthostis* and Parsis."[25] He cites the case of a Japanese mother who taught a daughter her Navjote prayers though the father was the Parsi of the family, and instances of Jugoslavian, Muslim, and Italian spouses far more involved than their Zoroastrian partners in Association activities. So inclusive, apparently, is his own Society that it approves "perform[ing] the *navjote* of a child irrespective of whether the parents are non-Parsis or Zoroastrians; . . . it is immaterial."[26]

What is happening here is that "membership" is coming to be defined by commitment and participation, and not by inherited identity. Pavri, and apparently a broad spectrum of his confreres, have been led by experience to an insight familiar to every student of psychology or sociology who examines the Troeltschian "church-denomination-sect" typology: that personal decision about what one wants to be and do is in most instances far more determinative than heredity in defining true identity, for it is grounded in conviction and imple-

[24]Information from Cyrus P. Mehta, May 1973.
[25]Pavri, *op.cit.*
[26]*Ibid.*

mented with zeal, whereas mere habits acquired by the "accident" of birth and inheritance may be left unexamined and without value in the formation of character. In short, converts may be a faith's most stalwart apologists. Understandably, the traditionalists cannot believe this, since their closed-door policy excludes the persons who could constitute the evidence. On the other hand, it may be too early to know whether or not an open-door policy will lead to compromises which sacrifice clarity about essentials. In any case, the concern of the traditionalists is that the name could be saved but the substance of their religion lost.

Cultic Issues

There is no question but that in recent years the traditional cultus has undergone alteration more rapidly and in greater measure than at any time in the religion's history. Though there were times in the past when ritual practices seemed all but extinguished, substantial restorations were effected, as for example by the Sasanians in Iran and, in India, by the Parsis (as instructed by the *Rivayats*). But the speed and ubiquity of twentieth century social change has sharpened and magnified several issues which need resolution. Actually, their resolution can hardly be avoided. The only question is whether the resolution is to be the consequence of rationally discussed and planned action or of malaise and default.

Of first importance is the issue of the proper shape, place, and role of ritual in the religion. Historically, it has been central and preoccupying in Zoroastrianism. It had its origin in a pastoral culture and its elaboration in a time when an ever increasing number of Iranians were engaged in agricultural pursuits. Its ideational base was thought about the world which yielded polytheistic conceptions generously laced with anthropomorphism.

The structure of the cultus was of a piece with the cultural setting and its pre-philosophical thought forms. The rites were thought to please the divinities who, in turn, would come down and manifest their power in the physical world, blessing worshipers with material boons. The priests who, in the last phases of the main formative period had established a hereditary monopoly of control over the religion, busied themselves with "culticizing" daily life and virtually all its activities and in both proliferating and refining the mechanics of ritual to guarantee its efficacy by punctilious correctness. The artifacts which served as symbols and as offerings were, of course, precisely those which would be familiar in a pastoral-agrarian age: mainly fire, water, goat's milk, bread, the pomegranate, date palm leaves, haoma juice, bovine urine and hair, fruits and nuts of the region.

Some hundreds of years later, what is remarkable is how little the cultus has been altered and, when altered, in what way. Resistance to change is shown by retention of almost the whole list of artifacts, the pattern of the daily Yasna ceremony in every adequately staffed fire-temple, the liturgical use of archaic languages exclusively, the five-times-daily kindling of first and second grade fires, the insistence upon the priests' purity (so conceived that cultic and physical cleanliness are confusedly mingled), and the hereditary principle of the priesthood. There are some rites that lost their existential reference {as times changed and have been forgotten, and a number of changes made to simplify the many retained. But these exceptions amount only to a few skipped measures in the old traditional tunes.

Yet, the Zoroastrians themselves have as a majority exchanged agrarianism for urbanization, and therein lies a clue as to *what* has changed. If it is not substance, form, or objective of the cultus, then what is it? The change is in the amount of heed paid to it. Inner ceremonies have never been corporate congregational rites, but their performance was traditionally supported by gratuities for dedicating them to the donors' desired ends. Now, priestly poverty pays mute witness to the laity's waning interest in commissioning ceremonies. New fire-temples are rarities; the down-grading of a fire-temple to dadgah rank is more common, since it reduces the need for priests as fire tenders.[27] The continuing decline of interest in training for the full time priesthood is another factor directly related to the neglect of the cultus, for the number and frequency of inner ceremonies can only shrink as the supply of priests diminishes. The residue consists mainly, therefore, of Navjotes, weddings, funeral rites and anniversary Afringans, and the Muktad celebrations on the final days of the year—all of them outer ceremonies and of a kind which for the most part, friends may attend along with the celebrants.

Yet only the problem has been stated. It becomes a critical and controversial issue because of differences of opinion about the response to make to it. The orthodox traditionalists, while recognizing the complete irrelevance of many ancient rites and therefore resign-

[27]See *supra*, p. 52.

ing themselves to such abridgment of the cultus as is *fait accompli*, are staunch in their conviction that the alternative to neglect of what remains is not a radical reconstruction but simply a dedicated reaffirmation of its traditional meaning and fidelity in its practice. If the community is declining and its survival is threatened, one good reason for it, they insist, is that the benefits inherent in rites are not appropriated. "To the extent we discard our time-honoured '*Rites*'," asserts Pithavala, "the moral fibre of our community will deteriorate in the same proportion and the '*Right*' way of life will also depart. The rot has already set in . . . "[28]

A major plank in the traditionalist platform is the retention of all the Avestan prayers and recitation in their original language. As Vimadalal expresses it, "These Manthras are a protection . . . from superphysical evil influence . . . also from any physical evil or misfortune or difficulty in this mundane world." The reformist Parsis who want to substitute modern languages are wrong.

> . . . they forget the power of sound, they forget that these prayers were composed not by ordinary men . . . but by seers and sages to whose vision the effect of these Manthras was open.
> . . . any attempt to substitute Gujarati must be nipped in the bud, for it would certainly be an evil day when this suicidal step is taken; it would toll the knell of our age-long connection with our ancient traditions, our glories and our ancestors, our religious rites, ceremonies and prayers.[29]

Dabu is found to be in full agreement. Parsis should use the exact words the Prophet and his apostles used because ". . . these are considered to be sacred and powerful incantations, used by the Magi, who knew the art of composing potent spells."[30]

---

[28]Behram D. Pithavala, "Era of Lord Zarathushtra," *Memorial Volume,* Golden Jubilee, *op. cit.,* p. 184.

[29]Jal Rustamji Vimadalal, "Power of Prayer," *Memorial Volume, ibid.,* pp. 6-8. The author's credentials were those of a Justice—i.e., a Judge of Bombay's High Court.

[30]Dabu, *Message of Zarathushtra, op. cit.,* p. 174. Kotwal and Boyd, in their earlier cited article, say, "The conception underlying this sacred speech [the chanted Avesta] is that there is a metaphysical correspondence between the sound uttered and the reality it signifies . . . the proper and righteous utterance of the Avesta invokes that reality." (p. 38).

Reformist sentiments vary with respect to the measure {of change that is thought needful; at the same time, all agree that the practice of the traditional cultus in the modern world is largely irrelevant. There are those who still appreciate the esthetic aspects of an earnest and skilled priest's chanting, but they go on to urge that Zoroastrians be educated in the meaning of the Avestan texts by studying them in translation. This, however, is a strategy that can lead to the unexpected consequence of complete disenchantment with the texts' content. Vajifdar has cited the instance of Dhalla, the historian, who once in his youth commissioned the performance of the Vendidad, then later learned its content and realizing "his folly . . . never had the ceremony performed again."[31]

Vajifdar, himself an author of a collection of prayers in English, characterizes priests as "unfortunate relics" and the cultus as an "obsolete system" which will probably not be changed "until it dies a natural death." Agreeing with the prophecies that there "may be no mobeds left in twenty years," he looks forward to the time when Zoroastrians "eventually learn to pray what the heart feels and yearns."[32]

That time seems even nearer in Iran than in Parsi India. As Boyce has found, tradition is holding its own in but a small number of isolated villages in the interior.[33] But the exodus of youth to cities and other countries and the disinterest of priests' sons in the priestly vocation provide together an impetus to simplify and rationalize the cultus, and to depend increasingly upon the laity for aid in performance of its more modest rubrics.

As for the Western communities, they are already following a pattern that will probably eventually prevail everywhere. In newsletters, journal articles, and correspondence, they express their shared interest in the "plight of the poor priests" and the conviction that the vocation should be markedly redefined. But one searches in vain for any hint of regret that their community resources do not permit the establishment of consecrated fire-temples and the installation of the staff of full time priests that would be the necessary corollary. The laity show every sign of being content with having

[31]Noshir H. Vajifdar, "Unfortunate Relics." *Parsiana*, June-September 1976, p. 41.

[32]*Ibid.*

[33]See Mary Boyce, *A Persian Stronghold of Zoroastrianism* (Oxford: Oxford University Press, 1977).

a place to gather, a few mobeds available to perform the congregational outer ceremonies for special occasions, and most of the responsibility for a policy that emphasizes education and the cultivation
of a sense of community rather than rites. It almost goes without
saying that they are in the vanguard of those insisting that a literature, both old and new, should be available in the language of their
common life. Driven to choose between resources that inform and
impart values and those which by mysterious "manthric power" are
supposed to bring divine influences to bear upon human problems,
they are choosing the former.

Among cultic issues, one requiring its own individual attention is
that of the dakhmas. The precise origin of the practice of exposure
as the means of disposing of the dead is obscure. The elaborate
justification of its cultic necessity, however, has long been a part of
the record, together with complex strategies for protecting the living
from being contaminated by the dead. Yet, for some time now,
many Zoroastrians have been bowing to the necessity of doing without dakhmas, or even, in most recent times, professing a preference
for cremation or burial.

The departures from the tradition for necessity's sake have been
made by those Parsis who have fanned out in India to form new
communities in various developing cities, yet in numbers too few to
afford the construction of dakhmas. Another factor is the unwillingness of persons nowadays to adopt the profession of preparing the
dead for disposal and bearing them to the dakhmas. They may
find some comfort in the community's pious expressions of high
regard for their valued services, but the resistance of the grateful
beneficiaries to associating with them in daily life makes them feel
that they are a caste of untouchables.

Abroad, Zoroastrians abide as a matter of course with the regulatory laws of their adopted lands and seek privacy of resting place
for their dead only if they can afford their own cemeteries. This is
the course now followed in Iran as well. Having already discarded
as archaic superstitions the ancient cultic tabus designed to protect
the living from pollution, Iranian Zoroastrians found no compelling
reason for continuing to use the dakhmas, particularly when their
abandonment ended a practice which the Muslim majority in Iran
had always disdained.[34]

[34]Iranian informants say that burial finally became the standard procedure in

A cultic practice essentially unique to Zoroastrianism thus has its own days numbered, and the only really remarkable phenomenon associated with its slow passing is the radical dichotomy in attitude about it. If it is a cause for grief in the communities where cremation or burial is the rule, that grief is too little to be seen or heard. Yet the slightest questioning of the traditional practice appearing in a publication read by Parsis in Gujarat or Bombay still evokes a choleric response the volume, intensity, and duration of which practically no other issue can arouse. Cremation is condemned on the ground that the electrical heat might be great enough to break into flame, and that would pollute fire. A faulty crypt may fail fully to seal decaying matter off from the surrounding soil, and thus permit pollution of earth. Either would be a grievous sin for which whoever of the living made the arrangements would be guilty. Curiously, however, there seems to be no dissolution of close relationships between partisans of tradition in Parsi-land and those who deviate from it by necessity abroad. Like the legalist dogmatists of some other religions, those of Zoroastrianism are not without the ability to hold their absolutist position in delicate balance with its opposite, the principle of Shayest-ne-shayest, permitting the bending of practice according to the prevailing circumstances.

The Underlying Problem

Most of the Zoroastrians' problems whether social, economic, ethical, or religious bear similarities to those which have confronted (or presently confront) other communities possessing the national, ethnic, or religious homogeneity essential to identity. What lends distinction to them, however, is the fact that they trouble a community which has shrunk in size to a critical point. Every problem, on this account, can be seen as a threat not only to the quality of some aspect of the Zoroastrians' lives but as one posing a danger to their ability to survive at all. The very real possibility of their extinction is always in their consciousness, heightening the poignancy and urgency of each individual concern.

Given the ultimacy and finality of what is feared, the question arises as to why every resource is not marshaled in support of active,

---

1966, although they could not be sure, they said, that there had not continued to be rare instances of exposure-by-dakhma in remote and isolated village areas.

concerted attacks on every subsidiary problem. The answer is already provided in detail in the chapter on institutional structure. Whatever the agency or institutional instrumentality devised for meeting some need or furthering some cause, it seems always that it is ultimately controlled by authority other than that of its members or officers. The name of that authority is tradition, an amorphous body of beliefs and practices of great but varying age, some contradicting others and therefore leading to differences of opinion and conviction, but always lying ready for reference as reason why any proposal to do what has not been done before can not be done.

The principal lack is that of a central representative, and overarching governing agency with constitutional powers to define policies agreed to by some reasonable majority of the delegated representatives, and to implement them by deciding the actions to be taken.

The present ways of handling problems resolve them piecemeal and to no one's satisfaction. Persons eager for meaning and renewal but frustrated by being told that they should practice more arduously what they have found meaningless, choose to drift and to let what they oppose grow weaker by neglect.

Migrant Zoroastrians forming the new communities are creating their own organizational structures with mechanisms for decision making. Their developing programs of religious education and nurture include materials suitable for each age group. Their problem is that their resources are not yet the equal of their vision and zeal. The Iranis have been doing the same, and in cities such as Tehran and Shiraz, they have had resources for it as well. But their problem is that they lack external guarantees of security by the society as a whole for working out their own destiny.

Finally, the way of those most obligated and yet least responsible—i.e., the way of the Parsis in India—is to talk. "Everybody talks: no one does anything," the late Lady Hirabai Jehangir remarked drily when asked, as the then President of the Parsi Panchayat of Bombay, for a diagnosis of what ailed the community. "Their vaunted unity is not the unity of agreement," she added, "but that of quarrelsomeness."[35]

---

[35]Interview with the late Lady Hirabai Jehangir, November 18, 1971. Genteel dowager though she was, Lady Jehangir could conclude sweetly reasoned discourse with blunt and pithy comment.

Recent developments underline her remarks. The influential trustees of the Panchayat in Bombay were successful in making the holding of the Third World Zoroastrian Congress (in January 1978) conditional upon its confining itself to discussion of problems and suggestions for improvement. The Congress could exercise no power either to define policy or to initiate action other than to recommend the formation of a broad-based educational committee and delegate the planning of the next Congress to the Federation of Parsi Zoroastrian Anjumans of India. But, as though the Panchayat had only waited until the delegations reached home, it cast its shadow across the path earlier lighted by at least the dim hope of making more progress at a fourth World Congress. Its means was that of withdrawing from the Indian Federation on the grounds that it had not served "any useful purpose."[36]

In a subsidiary resolution, the trustees promised to "take all such steps as may be necessary to establish and maintain links with Zoroastrian organisations all over the world, as contemplated during the deliberations of the IIIrd World Zoroastrian Congress in Bombay."[37]

Prophetically, *Parsiana* had gone to the heart of the Zoroastrian world community's problem in an issue of December 1977—before the Third Congress had even been convened—when it identified "the controversial question" as *the* controversial question! In other words, the proposal to debate a controversial issue is always killed by unresolved controversy over whether such an issue may be debated, much less moved toward resolution. The Panchayat's actions seem calculated to perpetuate this tradition.

On the other hand, the tradition may find itself challenged by a new World Zoroastrian Organization. Frustrated by the fragmentation and inaction of their world community, Londoners of the Zoroastrian Trust Funds of Europe took the initiative in inviting influential Zoroastrians of India, Iran, Australia, and the United States to the meeting (in July, 1980) at which the "WZO" was launched.[38] Its several aims emphasize amelioration of problems, encouragement of philanthropy to meet emerging needs, and the

[36]The full "Text of [the] Punchayat Resolution" was carried by *Parsiana* in its issue of February 1978, p. 3.

[37]*Ibid.*

[38]See *The Bombay Samachar* of August 10, 1980.

urgency of promoting religious education with a planned program of research and publication. These are familiar objectives, but the effort to widen and intensify concern and support for them is new. Moreover, the membership plan is one that invites panchayats or anjumans (associations) as well as individual Zoroastrians to join. It is the inclusion of associations which, implying commitment to representative democracy, could lead eventually to definitions of well-considered and widely-applicable policies that would serve the cause of renewal for the religion and assure its future. Many a Zoroastrian may consider commissioning the dedication of a Yasna ceremony to such a hope !

A BRIEF EPILOGUE

As the working of a Divine Providence has oft revealed, the will to move forward creatively and constructively can be strengthened more by preliminary defeat than by easy but minor achievement. The Zoroastrians may have temporized when they met up with niggling problems, but confronted by crises, they have surmounted them.

While it would be a mistake to predict that Zoroastrians will either now or always and forever "overcome," it is not an exaggeration to insist that they possess the traits essential to doing so if they but have the courage and the will to apply them in battle. They are intelligent and they are educated. They are compassionate and altruistic. There is sincerity in their piety and reverence and a stubborn insistence that it is better to be honest and good in this world than to make their way in it by wile and cleverness. They are also immensely sociable. They love sharing their good times. And they have style.

Long may they live.

Bibliography

Bharucha, Sheriarji Dadabhai. *A Brief Sketch of the Zoroastrian Religion and Customs.* Bombay: D.B. Taraporevala Sons & Co., 1928.

Bode, Framroze A. *Sharing the Joy of Learning.* Bombay: P.N. Mehta Education Trust, 1978.

Boyce, Mary. "Haoma, Priest of the Sacrifice," *W. B. Henning Memorial Volume.* Edited by Mary Boyce and Ilya Gershevitch. London: Asia Major Library, Lund Humphries, 1970.

——————. *The History of Zoroastrianism.* Vol. I. Leiden: E.J. Brill, 1975.

——————. *"A Last Stronghold of Traditional Zoroastrianism."* No. 7 of Teaching Aids for the Study of Inner Asia. Bloomington: Indiana University, 1977 (mimeographed).

——————. *A Persian Stronghold of Zoroastrianism.* Oxford: Oxford University Press, 1977.

——————. "Zoroaster the Priest," *Bulletin of the School of Oriental and African Studies,* XXXIII, Part I, 1970.

——————. "Zoroastrianism," *Religions of the Present.* Vol. II of *Historia Religionum.* Edited by C. Jouco Bleeker and Geo. Widengren. Leiden: E.J. Brill, 1971.

Boyd, James W., and Crosby, Donald A. "Is Zoroastrianism Dualistic Or Monotheistic?" *Journal of the American Academy of Religion,* XLVII/4, 1979.

Bulsara, J.F. "Social Reform Among the Parsis," *The Evelyn Hersey Memorial Lectures—1968.* Delhi: University of Delhi School of Social Work, 1968.

Bulsara, P.P. *Highlights of Parsi History.* Bombay: P.P. Bulsara, 1963.

Cama, Dara J. D. *We Parsis, Our Prophet, and Our Priests.* Bombay, 1966.

Chiniwalla, Framroze Sorabji. *Essential Origins of Zoroastrianism: Some Glimpses of the Mazdayasni Zarathosti Daen in its Original Native Light of Khshnoom.* Bombay: The Parsi Vegetarian and Temperance Society of Bombay, 1942.

Dabu, Khurshed S. *A Hand-Book of Information on Zoroastrianism.* Bombay: P.N. Mehta Educational Trust, 1969.

——————. *Message of Zarathushtra.* 2nd ed. Bombay: The New Book Co., 1959.

——————. *Zarathushtra and His Teachings.* Bombay: R.M.D. Chamarbaugvala, 1966.

Dawson, Miles Menander. *The Ethical Religion of Zoroaster.* New York: AMS Press, 1969 (reprinted from the edition of 1931).

de Bary, Wm. Theodore, *et al.* (compilers). *Sources of Indian Tradition.* Vol. LVI of *Records of Civilization, Sources and Studies.* Edited by Jacques Barzun. New York: Columbia University Press, 1958.

Desai, Sapur Faredun. *A Community at the Cross-Road.* Bombay: New Book Co., 1948.

_____. *The Parsi, Panchayet and its Working.* A Synoptic Survey, Revised and Enlarged. Bombay: 1963.

Dhabhar, Bamanji Nusserwanji (ed). *The Persian Rivayats of Hormazyar Framarz and Others.* Bombay: K.R. Cama Oriental Institute, 1932.

Dhalla, Maneckji Nusservanji. *History of Zoroastrianism.* New York: Oxford University Press, 1938.

Duchesne-Guillemin, Jacques. *Symbols and Values in Zoroastrianism.* Vol. 15 of *Religious Perspectives.* Edited by Ruth Nanda Anshen. New York: Harper and Row, 1966.

Geldner, Karl F. "Avesta Literature," *Avesta, Pahlavi, and Ancient Persian Studies,* First Series. Edited by Karl J. Trubner and Otto Harassowitz. Strassburg, 1904.

Ghirshman, R. *Iran.* Penguin Books, edition of 1954.

Homji, Homi B. Minocher. *O Whither Parsis ? Placate and Perish or Reform and Flourish ? A Study of Community Introspection.* Karachi, 1978.

Insler, S. *The Gathas of Zarathustra.* Vol. I, *Textes and Memoires,* No. 8 *Acta Iranica.* Leiden: E.J. Brill, 1975.

Iran Almanac and Book of Facts, 1977. 16th ed. Tehran: The Echo of Iran, Publisher, 1977.

Jackson, A.V. Williams. *Zoroaster, The Prophet of Ancient Iran.* New York: Columbia University Press, 1898.

Jungalwalla, Piloo. "The Navjote Ceremony," *Parsiana,* April-July 1975 (see Nanavutty).

Kanga, Maneck F. (ed.). *Citak Handarz I. Poryotkesan.* Bombay, 1960.

_____. "The Concept of an Ideal Priest," *Iran Society Silver Jubilee Souvenir Volume 1944-1969.* Calcutta: Iran Society, 1970.

Karaka, Dosabhai Framji. *History of the Parsis.* 2 vols. London: Macmillan and Co., 1884.

Karkhanavala, M.D. "Parsis, be true Mazdayasnian-Zarathostis," *Memorial Volume,* Golden Jubilee of the Memorial Column at Sanjan 1920-1971, etc. Edited by N.E. Turel and K.C. Sheriar. Bombay: Zoroastrian Jashan Committee, 1971.

Kotwal, Firoze M., and Boyd, James W. "The Zoroastrian paragna ritual," *The Journal of Mithraic Studies,* Vol. II; No. 1, 1977.

Kulke, Eckehard. *The Parsees: A Bibliography on an Indian Minority.* Freiburg, February, 1968.

_____. *The Parsees in India.* Delhi: Vikas Publishing House, 1974.

Mahoney, Pervin. "The Sound of Silence," *Parsiana,* June-July 1974.

Marker, Sanober. "Dini Avaz," *Parsiana,* February 1976.

. "The Plight of the Priests," *Parsiana,* November 1975.

Marshall, Ratan Rustomji. "Parsi Population Problem," *Rahe Asha.* Published by the Federation of the Parsi Zoroastrian Anjumans of India, June 1977.

Masani, Rustom. *Zoroastrianism: The Religion of the Good Life.* USA: The Macmillan Company, 1968.

Mirza, H.K. "On Conversion and Converts in Zoroastrianism," *Parsiana,*

August, 1970.

Moddie, Asphandiar D. "Impressions of the Third World Zoroastrian Congress," *Parsiana*, March 1978.

Modi, Jivanji Jamshedji. "The Parsi Priesthood," *Journal of the K.R. Cama Oriental Institute*, Vol. XXXI, 1937.

_____. *The Religious Ceremonies and Customs of the Parsees*. Bombay: British India Press, 1922.

Moulton, James Hope. *Early Zoroastrianism*. London: Williams and Norgate, 1913.

_____. *The Treasure of the Magi*. London: Oxford University Press, 1917.

Naigamwalla, Naval Kavasjee D. (compiler). *Zarathushtra's Glorious Faith: Zoroastrianism and Its Followers, the Parsis*. Poona, 1967.

Nanavutty, Piloo (Jungalwalla). *The Parsis*. New Delhi: National Book Trust, India, 1977.

Olmstead, A.T. *History of the Persian Empire*. Chicago: The University of Chicago Press, 1948.

Pavry, Jal Dastur Cursetji. *The Zoroastrian Doctrine of a Future Life*, 2nd ed. Vol. Eleven of the *Columbia University Indo-Iranian Series*. Edited by A.V.W. Jackson. New York: AMS Press, 1965.

Paymaster, Feroza. "Would you Marry out of the Community ?" *Parsiana*, December-January 1975.

Peer, Peshotan F. "The Zoroastrian Priesthood," Third World Zoroastrian Congress Paper, abridged. *Parsiana*, August-November 1978.

Pithawala, Behram, E. "Era of Lord Zarathushtra—As deciphered from the letters in his Holy Name," *Memorial Volume, op cit.*, 1971.

Ranina, Jehangir M. "We Parsis," *Parsiana*, February 1969.

Report for the year 1970, Trustees of the Parsi Punchayet Funds and Properties Bombay.

Schmidt, Hanns-Peter. "Zarathustra's Religion and His Pastoral Imagery," Reprint of lecture delivered on the occasion of his inauguration as Professor of Sanskrit at the University of Leiden, June 6, 1975.

Tavaria, P.N. "Khshnoom," *Parsiana* February 1966.

_____. "Talismanic 81,000," *Parsiana*, May 1966.

_____. "Khshnoom: Numerological Expression." *Parsiana*, November 1966.

_____. "Khshnoom: 'Nirarg,' " *Parsiana*, April 1967.

Umrigar, K.D. "Are the Parsis Dying Out?" *The Illustrated Weekly of India*, August 29, 1971.

Vajifdar, Noshir H. "Unfortunate Relics," *Parsiana*, June-September 1976.

Vimadalal, Jal Rustamji. "Power of Prayer," *Memorial Volume, op cit.*, 1971.

_____. *What a Parsee Should Know*. Bombay: Justice Vimadalal, 1967.

Wadia, P.A., *et al*. *Parsis Ere the Shadows Thicken*. Bombay: P.A. Wadia, 1949.

Zaehner, R. C. *The Dawn and Twilight of Zoroastrianism*. New York: G.P. Putnam's Sons, 1961.

Miscellaneous Sources

Bombay Samachar, The, Editorials
"Judgment of the Hon'ble Mr. Justice Beaman, 27 November 1908," in the

Parsi Punchayet Case, Suit No. 689 of 1906.

Letters from Framroze A. Bode, Hollywood, California; Cyrus P. Mehta, London, England; Jamshed K. Pavri, Vancouver, Canada; T.R. Sethna, Karachi, Pakistan.

Minutes of the August 1977 Meeting of the Managing Committee of the F.M. Cama Athornan Institute and the M.M. Cama Education Committee.

Parsiana, Editorials and staff articles.

"Report of the Third World Zoroastrian Congres, 1978," (unpublished) by Lovji D. Cama, New York.

Index